AF323447

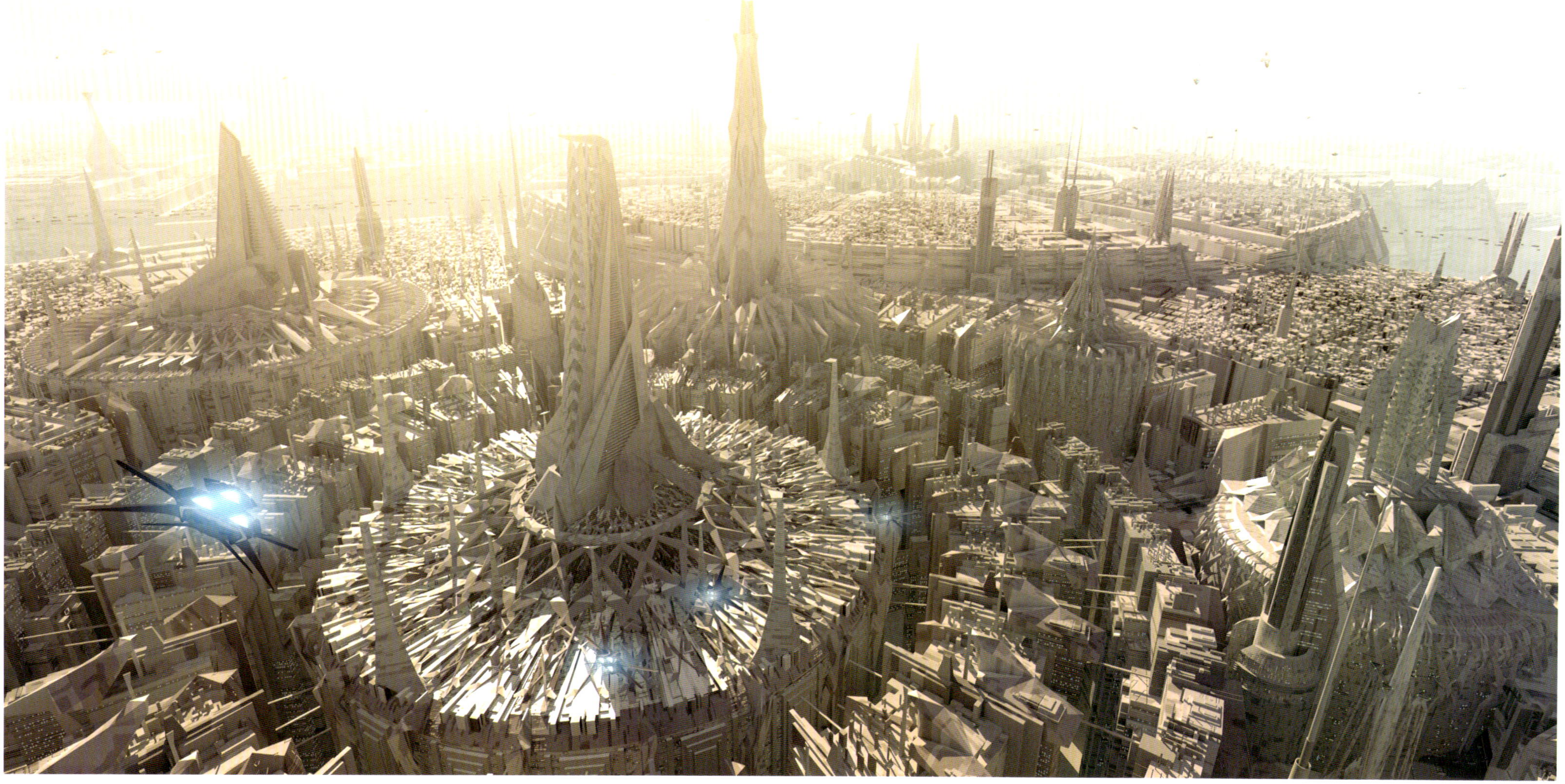

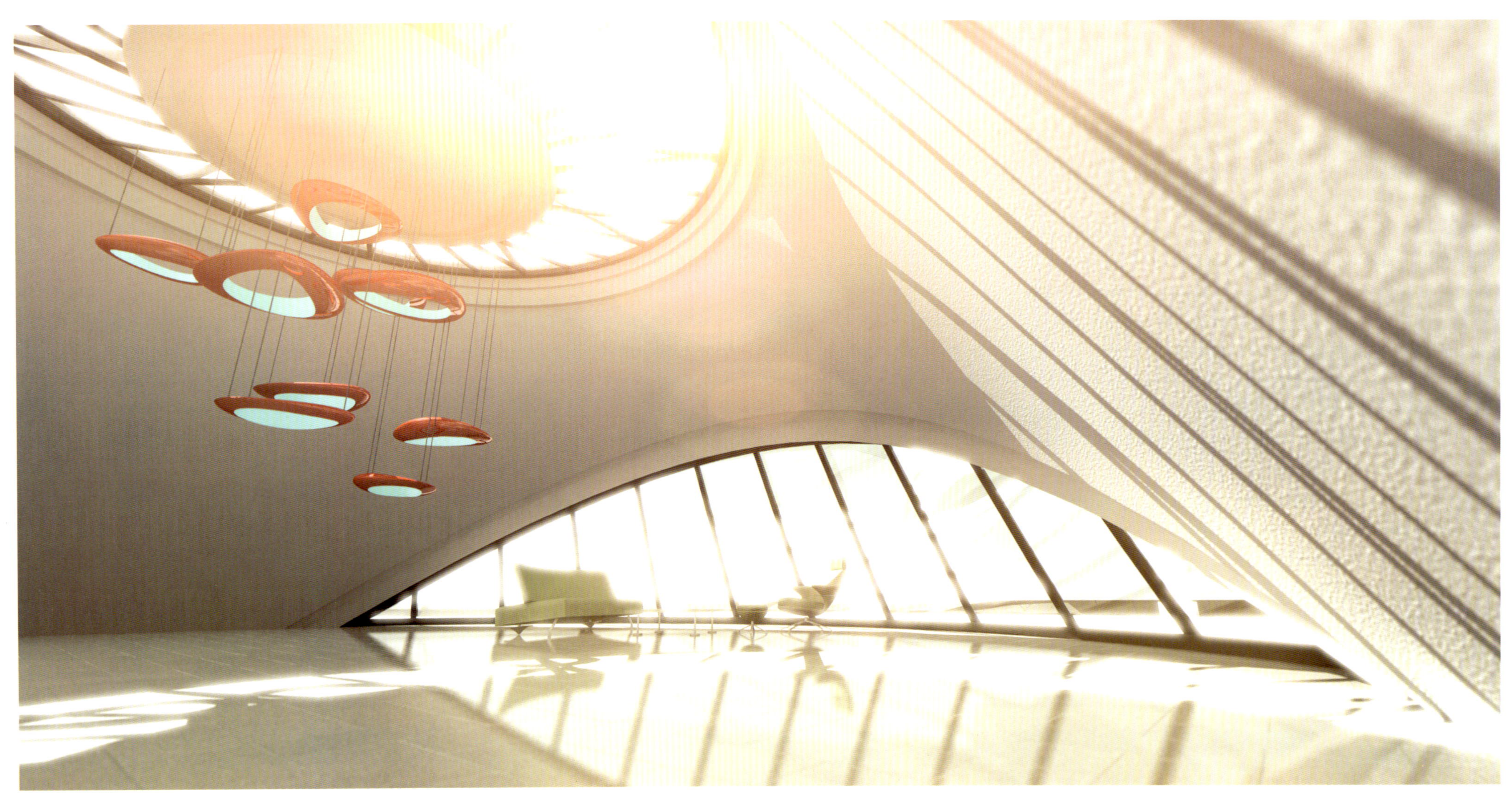

PLACES

SEÁN HARGREAVES

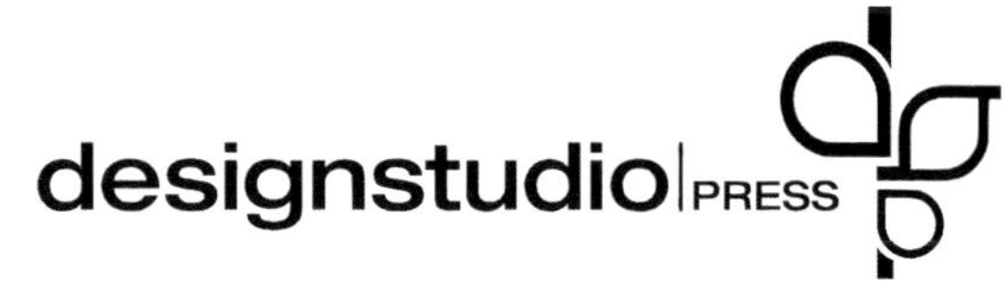

Imagination is more important than knowledge. For knowledge is limited to all we know now and understand, while imagination embraces the entire world, and all there ever will be to know and understand.

- ALBERT EINSTEIN

This book is dedicated to my wife Sandy, my mother and father Frances and Mike,
and my sister Rebecca.

Page 1:
CAEN
3000 x 1500 pixels

Page 2:
CONICULUS
3000 x 1500 pixels

CONTACT INFO:
Seán Hargreaves can be reached by e-mail at: **seanhargreaves1@me.com**
To see more of Seán's work visit: **www.seanhargreavesdesign.com**
He can also be found on Facebook (Seán Hargreaves or Seán Hargreaves Design)

Text Editor: Christina Apeles

Published by Design Studio Press
8577 Higuera Street
Culver City, CA 90232
Website: www.designstudiopress.com
E-mail: info@designstudiopress.com

10 9 8 7 6 5 4 3 2 1

Printed in China
First edition, October 2011

Hardcover ISBN 13: 978-1-933492-59-9

Paperback ISBN 13: 978-1-933492-49-0

Library of Congress Control Number:
2011927804

CONTENTS

FOREWORD *by Eric Saarinen, ASC*   08

FOREWORD *by Doug Trumbull*   10

INTRODUCTION   12

PHOTOSHOP WORK   14

ABSTRACTIONS   18

COMPUTERS   24

VEHICLES   32

ARCHITECTURE

     EXTERIORS   48

     INTERIORS   76

BIOGRAPHY   158

FOREWORD 1

by ERIC SAARINEN, ASC

I am the son of Eero and Lily Saarinen. My grandfather Eliel grew up in Finland and became a famous European architect. Among his many works in Finland was the Central Railroad Station in Helsinki. His wife, Loja, was a famous weaver, and they worked together on many projects. In 1925, George Booth, a mogul newspaperman, commissioned Eliel to design a campus called Cranbrook Academy of Art in Bloomfield Hills, Michigan. They emigrated there when my father was 15. Cranbrook was like a creative magnet. Many famous artists met and worked there. The faculty consisted of handpicked architects, artists, designers, sculptors, and weavers, and my grandfather became the academy's head. His philosophy was to design everything…from a city-planning scale, right down to the cutlery. At 15, my father, Eero, was also designing chairs for the girls' school, Kingswood, and some comic faces that were placed between the stones in the walls of Cranbrook. It was there my father met my mother, Lily, a sculptor who was studying under the famous Swedish sculptor Carl Milles. Charles and Ray Eames met my father and mother there and became best friends. The Eameses were my godparents. Frank Lloyd Wright bounced me on his knee, although my grandfather would love to say, "They called him Frank, but he wasn't always right."

This was where I came from. Art was God. That's all everyone talked about. To me, the architecture of Cranbrook was normal. Paintings were normal. Classical music was normal. That's all I knew.

Eliel and Eero competed against each other, each entering their own designs of the St. Louis Arch. My father won. He had also designed the Tulip table and chair, and the Womb chair for Knoll International. I remember being called in to sit in the Womb chair. It was the most comfortable chair I'd ever sat in. As a kid, I could sit on the arm, or completely curl up inside it. That's when I learned never to judge a chair before sitting in it. I also remember my dad dragging out the prototype for the Tulip chair. It was made of plasticine, so I couldn't sit in it, but that was 1948 or so, and although there wasn't anything like it at that time, I was frustrated because I couldn't sit in it. My mother's sculpture was extremely organic. When she was a child, she spent a lot of time going to the zoo drawing the animals. She understood organic form and worked at my father's office. Her work became very free form…like animals. She worked in clay, and I'm convinced that my father took some of these shapes and redid them in a much larger scale, with prestressed concrete.

The TWA building in New York looks like a bird from the top…extremely organic with very few straight lines. In any case, models were great learning tools for them. My father attributed his abilities to "97 percent hard work and 3 percent talent."

Eliel died in 1950. That was a big blow to everyone. My dad said later that in a way it set him free from working inside that "box." Over the course of ten years, my dad designed the GM Technical Center in Warren, John Deere headquarters in Moline, Bell Labs in Holmdel Township, Yale's Morse and Stiles Colleges and Ingalls Hockey Rink in New Haven, the Dulles Airport in Washington, the TWA terminal and CBS Building in New York City, the U.S. Embassy in London, the…well, let's just say he didn't spend too much time hanging out with me. He died in 1961. I was 19.

When my father was working on the Dulles Airport, he needed to sell the idea of the "Mobile Lounge" to the money people. It was a multimillion-dollar investment. The idea was that each passenger only had to walk 150 feet, and then they would step into a VIP lounge that had drinks and couches. Those days you could even smoke. You'd wait a few minutes and then the lounge backed away from the main terminal and went to the plane. It had a scissors lift underneath to lift itself up to the plane. My dad asked Charlie Eames to make a film to sell the lounge idea. I was in the same room when my father saw the results…a clever visual animation of a tree growing represented the airports those days. The bigger the jets, the longer the walks. We found ourselves walking for miles. In fact, in one year passengers were walking around the moon and back two and a half times. My father walked briskly past me, muttering, "Maybe I should have been a filmmaker." I never forgot that, and also realized it was a persuasive art form. It was like painting, but with the dimension of time. You could tell a story. I realized it was "fair game" for me to explore. I went to UCLA's film school.

I was a hippy in the '60s. Charles and Ray Eames took me under their wing. Over the years I've done several projects with them as a cameraman. The Eames office was a lot like my dad's office in Michigan. They both had "model shops." They both would make scale models to study and improve physical spaces. Charles and Ray inspired me to work on films. I loved it. I had found a fire inside me…something related to the arts.

I learned several big lessons. The first was to work as hard as I could. These grownups around me certainly did. Another lesson was to gather the best people in their field around me. I learned to use "models," just as my dad and the Eameses did. I ended up becoming successful as a director and cameraman for television commercials.

My production company had competed for and won a campaign for Land Rover that involved a 180-degree crane move, where every shot started upside down and ended up right side up, or vice versa. We had designed the crane to be modular, with its greatest length of 55 feet. It was designed to fit inside a Boeing 737 cargo container. We would fly country to country, starting in Bangkok and ending up in the US, having done eight shots, each shot lasting eight to 11 seconds. We had our tickets, had our shots...were ready to go.

Then the planes flew into the buildings on September 11, 2001. The car company wouldn't let us fly anywhere. I had to find the best production designer. I looked at hundreds of reels. That's how I met Seán Hargreaves. He had to recreate China, Africa, East Africa, South America, Thailand, a North American ferry crossing, and two more scenes, all within an hour of downtown Los Angeles. We never used blue screen, we never shot "elements," everything was done "in camera." We never used 3D imaging.

I'll never forget Seán getting a little agitated and saying, "Stop the car," on a scout one day near Palmdale, California, looking for "Africa." He said nothing...walked over to a tree, and then over toward a ridge... looked down and pondered for a while, and then came back to the car saying, "I think I've found Thailand." As a production designer, Seán is a "big vision guy." He inserted a 12-foot high Buddha head into the mud cliff on the ridge. We put a tent with a couple of Thai archeologists speaking Taiwanese, chipping away at archeological relics. Seán put a live monkey at the top of the tent...in the middle background we had a dozen or so Buddhist monks in their red robes walking down a trail. Behind that, on the horizon, we tacked some stock shots of Thai temples in the distance. We shot it at sunset. What a great shot that was! That was ten years ago.

Looking at this book, you can see what I mean by "a big vision guy." We worked on a number of jobs together. We traveled around Europe together...and had some great adventures. He was always interested in modern architecture. One time we were bidding on a job that had a lot to do with "big industry," and we chose Berlin, where there's quite a lot of new, interesting, organic architecture. But the wiser powers that be chose New Zealand, I'm sure because it was a little more "generic," which to us, meant boring!

There are not many people with the passion and ability to put this kind of book together. He studied at Art Center, which is a grueling, tortuous sharpening of the mind and head-first difficult assignments, where you work four hard years because there's just no time left for partying. We care about many of the same things. We're both passionate about our work, and I'd like to add that he's funny, charming, and, like most English, I suppose, they get their way not by direct force, but by sticking to their creative guns...never losing sight of their goal.

He sent me some of his images for the book. I'm amazed at the different styles and organic approaches. They remind me of my dad's work to some extent, and my relationship with him is a little like Eero's relationship with Charles Eames. When we're together we push each other. I love the way each design in his book is like him scrambling up a branch of a tree...just seeing where it takes him. But he doesn't stop. He'll climb every branch of that tree. Every tree on the hill. He's not copying anyone, he's not even copying himself, and the fire never goes out. I do think we all learn from our contemporaries and those who go before us...hey, we learn from nature too. Why not?

It has been my honor to have known and worked with Seán. Written on my grandfather's gravestone in Finland are the words "WORK IS THE KEY TO THE CREATIVE GROWTH OF THE MIND." I think Seán takes that to heart in these incredible visual landscapes and futuristic architectural designs.

Eric Saarinen, ASC
director

FOREWORD 2

by DOUG TRUMBULL

Seán Hargreaves's work has me completely convinced that he has already been to the future, and came back with some great snapshots of places I would really like to visit. There is hope, inspiration, optimism, and, above all, an artist's eye that finds light and atmosphere that make me believe.

Those qualities are hard to define, yet Seán seems to intuitively know how to light a design so that it glows with life and credibility. And the structures predict a future that seems overflowing with wild imaginary shapes, as well as industrial design materials and fabrication that I want to touch and feel. Gleaming plasteel and energy-infused metals morphed into devices, vehicles, buildings, and whole cities that are alive with a positive hope for the future.

Movies rarely go into that territory, because drama and conflict are the rule of the day, so something must be terribly wrong in order for a film to take the audience into crisis and resolution. Smoggy, polluted dystopias rule, and if something of the future is glimpsed through the eyes of a Sean Hargreaves, it will soon be flooded, detonated, or otherwise rendered impossible to sustain via some nuclear holocaust, plague, alien attack, or whatever those filmmakers can regurgitate.

I do not agree that crisis-driven melodrama is the only way to make a movie, and have worked a long time trying to depict a future vision that can compel us all to seek it out, design it, build it, drive it, live in it, and hopefully transform human nature by dragging us forward against our barbaric nature, to joyfully become welcome inhabitants of the universe. But this is not an easy task.

Ever since I had the great pleasure of working with Stanley Kubrick on his masterpiece, *2001: A Space Odyssey*, I have been hooked on the notion that movies could, over time, become even more powerful and enlightening about man's place in a universe filled with life, by employing ever more immersive media technologies to present awesome imagery that engulfs audiences in a sense of *being there*.

Seán is one of my antidotes, and I just keep looking at his images, hoping that one day we will work together to make a spectacle like none before, in a giant screen holographic phantasm of sensory stimulation that will cause the human genome to suddenly hit a tipping point—and become wise and compassionate.

Seán has worked on many movies and with a number of big name directors. They have been enormously lucky to partake of his talents. Yet the work is reduced to the screen and seen only in cramped multiplexes, and if they are in 3D they are dim as hell. What I have been working on, and making exciting progress with, is that new medium that can engulf audiences far more powerfully than the old Cinerama of *2001*, and even more exciting than the giant IMAX screens that have defined today's top-of-the-line movie experiences. If you have had the good fortune to see a real IMAX film shot in the original giant-frame 70 mm process and projected onto their largest 100-foot screens, you may have noticed that it is the profound visuals that carry the day, that shots last a long time so that you can savor every pixel of beauty, and that films about the International Space Station, elephants, or Mount Everest may, at best, use a famous actor as narrator. But the powerful and immersive imagery can sweep you up into another realm of appreciation for man's achievements, nature's wonder, and deliver a profound sense of optimism and enthusiasm to viewers. That is what Seán's amazing imagery does for me.

I am sure that you can imagine that seeing the amazing works in this book probably won't thrill you very much if you could only see them on your iPhone or laptop. But here in this book is pure Seán, unedited, and undiminished by anything other than paper and printer's ink. But on our giant holodeck of new projection technology, Seán's visions may soon be blasted onto your retinas and slammed into your visual cortex in such a way that mere words, melodrama, or movie clichés will pale by comparison.

Seán uses cutting-edge computer technology to realize his ideas, but he does not fall into the seductive embrace of clever algorithms that can rob an image of spark and life. The unexpected triumphs here, and a true artist is at work directing your attention, deftly controlling the depth of field like a seasoned cinematographer, and painting with light like an old master.

I am quite critical of computer-generated imagery, because much of the work I see looks somehow synthetic. That's not to say that there aren't many completely amazing visual effects being produced these days, including living creatures and even human beings that are almost alive. But Seán brings to this new art form something extra—life and passion. In movie production, talents like Seán are devoured into a production pipeline that often obscures their individual contribution, while vast teams of animators, compositors, art directors, and cinematographers massage the overall project into an apparently seamless whole. It often takes many hundreds of talented people to pull this off, and the work is often contracted to multiple "effects houses" to deliver the many shots required. And in the process, something that could be awesome is often reduced to adequate. CGI, as the synthesis is called, is a mix of artistry and mathematics. The images, however unique and effective, end up projected onto screens at 24 frames per second at relatively low brightness, because of antiquated industry standards as well as shortcomings of projector lamps, along with theatre managers trying to save on a few amps of power. And since 3D requires various filters or polarizers, the resultant brightness is only one quarter of previous industry standards. I think we all deserve better, and I know that Seán's work really shimmers and glows when it is seen under brilliant illumination. And on a giant hemispherical screen at a zillion frames per second, you will be right there inside Seán's amazing imagination.

I follow the world of architecture, and find Seán's ideas for shape and structure to be completely plausible, buildable, and inhabitable. It would be a wonderful thing if something he designs for a world of science fiction actually became real. I would like to help that idea along in a movie, because in films we also build full-scale sets, and we also build photorealistic miniatures. Since Seán works in CGI, that means there is actually a set of plans to inform real construction, whether via a computer-controlled milling machine or laser cutter, 3D prototyping, or myriad other technologies that can now enable actual physical construction of what at first appears to be impossible, fanciful, and fictional. That means we can go one more step beyond the limitations of a CGI rendering, which sometimes falls just a tiny bit short of complete realism, because the render time for each frame can become prohibitive if one does all the shaders, ray tracing, radiosity, global illumination, and other processes that require so much time—and money.

I enjoyed working with Ridley Scott and futurist Syd Mead on *Blade Runner*. They are both accomplished artists, with Ridley doing amazing drawings on napkins at dinner and Syd delivering masterful paintings. The film was dystopian, however, and it was *dark*. So the technical limitations of film and visual effects techniques did not diminish the film in any way. In fact, I would still do it much the same way today, but with digital compositing, rather than optical. Seán Hargreaves, however, is an optimistic futurist, and his images deliver the joy of light. Therefore we need a whole new medium of film, call it Hyperfilm, with brilliance, giant screens, high frame rates, and more—in order to deliver the full impact of what Seán can conceive. Let's do it!

Doug Trumbull
visual effects pioneer

INTRODUCTION

I believe that for artists and designers, images are born from the experiences one observes during the first ten to 15 years of their lives. Through time, those images are subconsciously refined over and over in one's life. They may consist of shapes or places or films...but they always stay present in the back of one's memory and now and then they make an appearance in an image or design that one creates.

For me, there are two important images that stand out from my childhood. One is of the green countryside of Stalmine in northern England, where I was raised as a child, and the other is of machines that I saw when I accompanied my father to factories during his business visits.

My father is an accomplished mechanical engineer and my mother has always been very creative. At a very young age, accuracy was always stressed in my drawings. I remember my father doing sketches for me to use as guides when I was drawing as a child. As I grew older, I became quite adept at reproducing exactly what I saw in a sketch. My parents continued to encourage my talent and around ten years old, I began to realize I had a special talent that I could use in the future. Over time, I continued to refine my designs; some are very detailed and some are very minimalist.

At the age of 13 my family moved to the United States. After we landed, my first image of the country was from the window of a Boeing 747 looking out to Washington Dulles Airport. The great architect Eero Saarinen designed the main building. As I watched, a bus-type vehicle came out to the airplane, lined itself up perpendicular to the aircraft, and then proceeded to rise up on legs to reach the height of the doorway. Then it slowly edged forward to attach itself to the plane and allow passengers to disembark, after which it slowly backed off, lowered itself to bus height, and went on its way to this beautiful building. At any age that would have been a sight to see, but at 13 it was a memory that has lodged itself forever in my frontal lobe.

When I was growing up, I remember looking at objects I never saw before, such as a machine. Not knowing what it was or did, it presented a mystery to me. There have been many times when I've seen a tool or machine and have asked, "What does it do?" Many times the explanation destroyed my fantasy of what it was, but I still continue to ask.

As a young boy in the countryside of northern England, I watched as my father designed and built our new family home. The house was very modern and different from all the other surrounding homes, and it was perfectly furnished with beautiful modern furniture from prominent designers from the mid-century period. The house, called Sunset Lodge, was built in an enclave of trees not visible from the road. Even as a child I was not blind to the fact that we had a very special place. It was a house that got people's attention. I attribute my upbringing in these surroundings to significantly influencing my designs to this day.

My first foray, and one may say apprenticeship, into design came at the age of 18 at an engineering company in Dallas, Texas. I worked there over the summer before starting college. There I learned about the prototype design phase from drafting to making models. The following summer I worked at an advertising agency where I worked on storyboards and layouts for print campaigns. During these jobs, my appreciation of aesthetics increased.

After graduating from Art Center College of Design, I worked at General Motors Advanced Concept Center designing concept cars. Through my work at ACC and through my experience in the entertainment industry, I was and still am surrounded by great talent of all kinds. I value working with accomplished artists and artisans in their crafts, and I feel it pushes me by learning from their expertise. However, I also believe, as a designer, invariably there comes a time when one gains enough experience and confidence in one's own abilities, and realizes it is possible to stop glancing at references from others, and go on to do your own designs.

As designers we are taught that sketching is an important part of the design process. The final image is the presentation of the refinement of all these sketches. When the final image is presented it is usually presented with all the sketches that led up to the final design. I've always agreed with this approach to a certain degree, but I have also questioned it. I feel there are "filtering" issues when sketching. By "filtering" I am referring to the sketches that follow the initial idea. Over time, sketching the design over and over may be refining it, but in many cases, the initial design is also being "watered down." As a result, the final design may end up being a mere long lost relative of the initial idea.

The designs in this book did not start out for a book at all, but as an exercise I laid out for myself. I wanted to create designs without any preconceived sketches, and in many cases not having any idea of the end result. I did away with sketches completely. I wanted to design as I was designing.

In 1998 I was working as a production designer at George Lucas's Industrial Light & Magic on a large multimillion-dollar ad campaign. One of the main elements I needed to design was a radical skyscraper, as it was an important image throughout the series of commercials in the campaign. My design for the skyscraper was made into a model and was presented to the ad agency. The head of the agency rejected the design on the grounds that it was too futuristic. This was on a Friday evening, and I needed to work the entire weekend on a new design for the tower so it would be ready to present on Monday morning.

Due to time constraints, we decided to come up with some ideas in 3D. I partnered with a CG modeler, and in six hours I had come up with a myriad of ideas for the design with the modeler's help in realizing them. There were no sketches involved except maybe a quick doodle here and there. We just dove in. I realized very quickly how in broad strokes a design could be developed in this manner. No longer was I sitting and sketching one design in three or four different angles and drawing the design over and over. We submitted the designs of the tower first thing Monday morning and one was chosen immediately.

Afterward, I thought about this experience a lot. Previously I had taught myself Vectorworks so that I could use the perspective as a guide to my renderings. For example, drawing an ellipse in perspective is very trying and time consuming, and ellipse guides favored by designers aren't in perspective. With 3D, I discovered a new way to present ideas and designs that could be seen in a myriad of accurate views, lighting conditions, and surfaces. I was eager and excited to use this new tool, so I taught myself to design using 3D software.

As a designer, I have always felt it important to render images that are clear and precise so that the viewer has a clear understanding of what one is seeing regardless if the medium is sketching, painting, marker rendering, or working in 3D. When an idea is presented and then the final design is approved to be built, it is then handed over to numerous people who will take the design to the finished product. These people need to interpret the idea as clearly as possible, so that there is no mistake, misinterpretation, or "watering down" of the design. One of the main aspects of 3D that I like is there is no faking the design. Due to the clarity of the 3D image, everything is right there for the viewer. Whether the design is good or bad is in many cases subjective, however, one has to at least understand clearly and concisely what one is looking at.

When designing environments, vehicles, architecture, or worlds, I find it useful to use a linear timeline. This timeline contains three sections of time: present, future, and super future. These sections of time can be dates used for reference. For instance, the future may be in 100 years, the super future could be 1,000 years from the present. I find this timeline helps quite a lot if you are designing an object in the future that already exists in the present. For example, take a car. We know what a car looks like now, but what will it look like in 100 years or 1,000 years? In the super future, maybe there will be teleprocess, and possibly the entire look of cities has changed, maybe there are no longer roads. By designing using a timeline as a guide, it allows an evolutionary projection through time. Periods can be added between the three sections. This type of design process for the most part does away with a design that "just looks good"—it reflects a solid thinking behind it. The design is developed through an evolutionary process, which may result in a revolutionary design.

For the designs in this book, the process led to some interesting results. In creating them I found I was designing in a different manner. Some of the designs were grown from one another, adding and subtracting from the design. Some of the images I directly reproduced from something in my head. With others, it was more of an organic search to see where I could go and how far I could push the software. I have presented the images as pure as my equipment allows. No photos were used, nothing is collaged, and only minor Photoshop work was used for some atmospherics and texture mapping.

The places you will see in this book are not highly populated. I am not a fan of crowds. The images reflect a certain silence. I prefer seeing a single person or a few people sitting or walking silently through complex or very minimal places. As you will see, there is a certain "look" in these designs, a look born from those places and things I've stored in my memory and have refined over time.

Seán Hargreaves
Los Angeles
2011

01

This was one of my early Photoshop illustrations. I planned and executed it traditionally, first drawing a thumbnail sketch, then enlarging that to an 11"x17" page and doing the tight line drawing in pencil, then again with a 0.05mm pen. Following that I scanned it and painted it. This file ended up being very large as I was painting at 500dpi. I worked all my perspective out in the thumbnail, using vanishing points that were about 3' apart for quite a small sketch. I've always liked photography taken with long lenses, so a lot of my traditional illustrations were designed that way, but that alone gave me problems due to the vanishing points being so far apart, using very long rulers even for the smaller items in an image, such as the many frames hanging in this room.

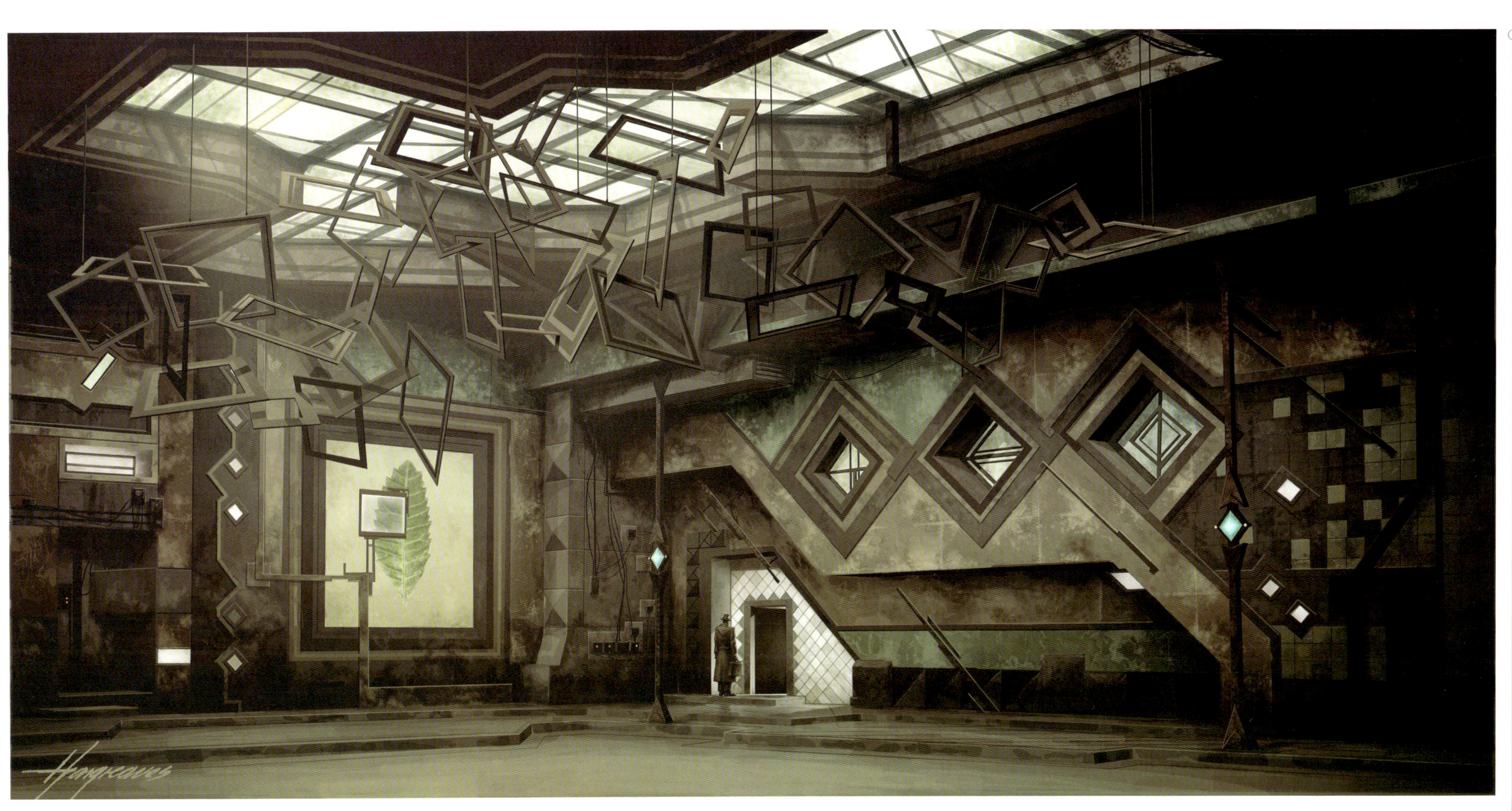

OHM - 4

13500 x 7011 pixels

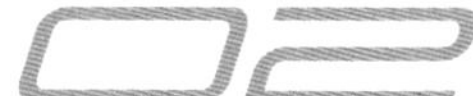

This was the last fully digital painting I did before concentrating on using 3D software. As in the previous illustration, *Ohm-4*, it's a look into an underground city, but one that is somewhat claustrophobic in its scale with its narrow corridors, low ceilings, and patches of dim light. I also like little art motifs and unusual detailing such as here on the walls.

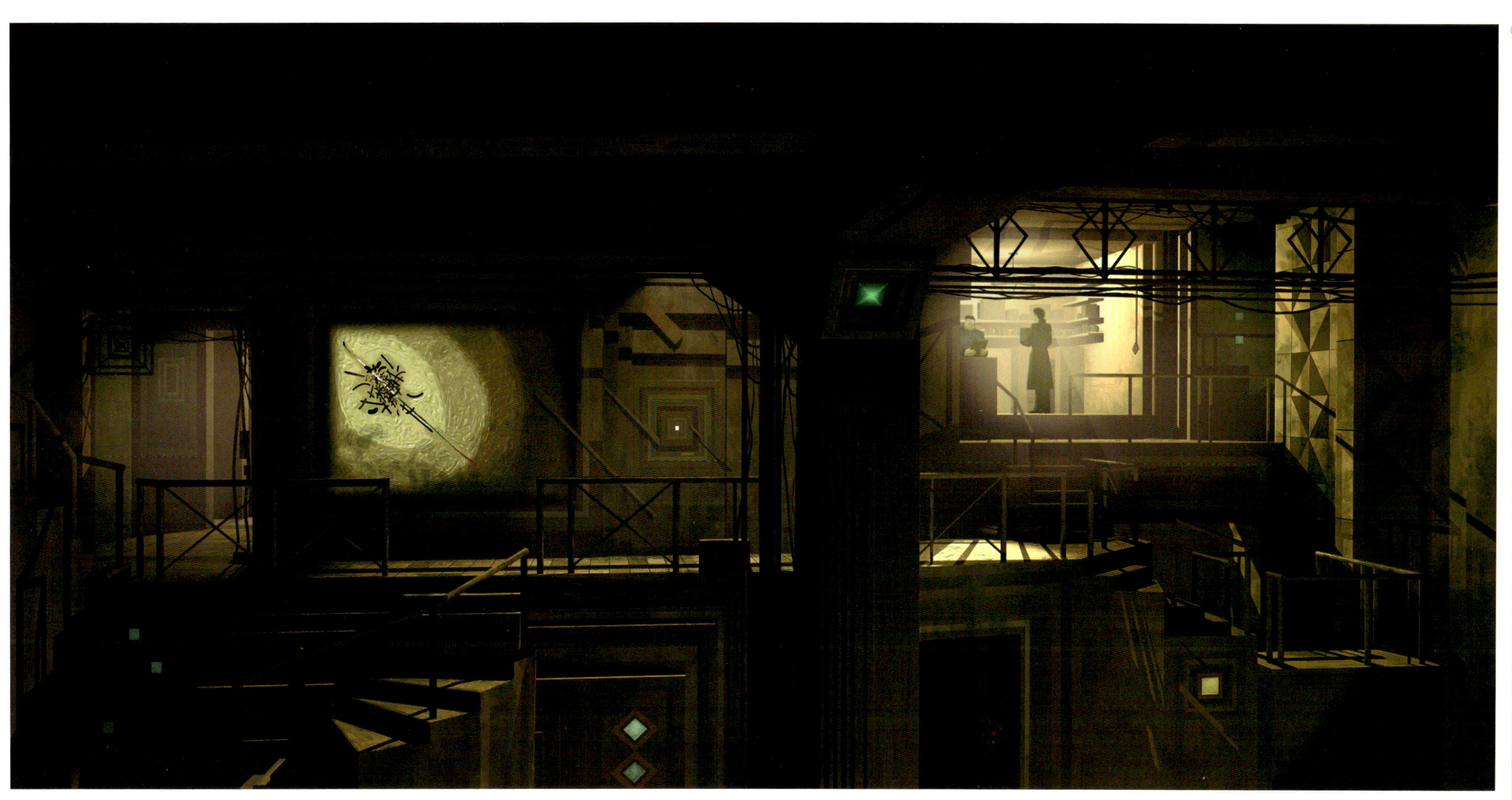

UNDWELLUM
5100 x 2550 pixels

ABSTRACTIONS

I started doing abstract pieces as a study for pushing shapes to their ultimate without breaking the polygons. I found amazing and beautiful shapes could be made, and I concentrated on shapes that transcended things I've seen.

Abstractions have crept into architecture quite significantly in the past decade. Random algorithms have produced shapes that look like they are "grown," and are very organic, some very much like plants.

I love abstract sculpture. In my first year at university I had to sculpt an abstract shape out of soapstone, and once I was finished I was exhausted. I wanted instant results and sculpting stone of any kind isn't fast. I have a great appreciation for sculptors, the materials they carve, their patience, and vision.

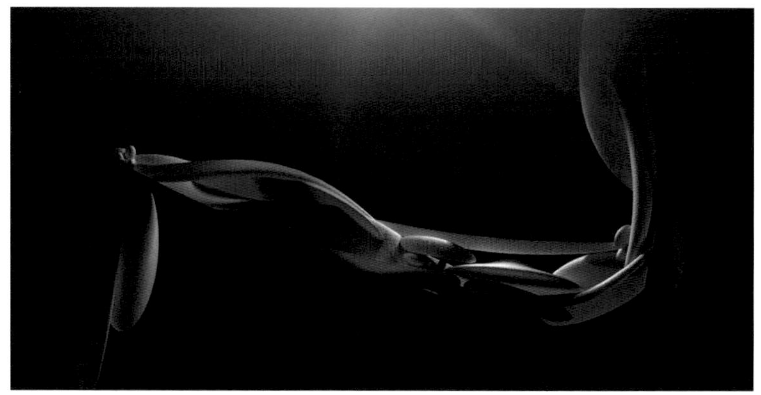

ABSSTRACT 2
1024 x 515 pixels

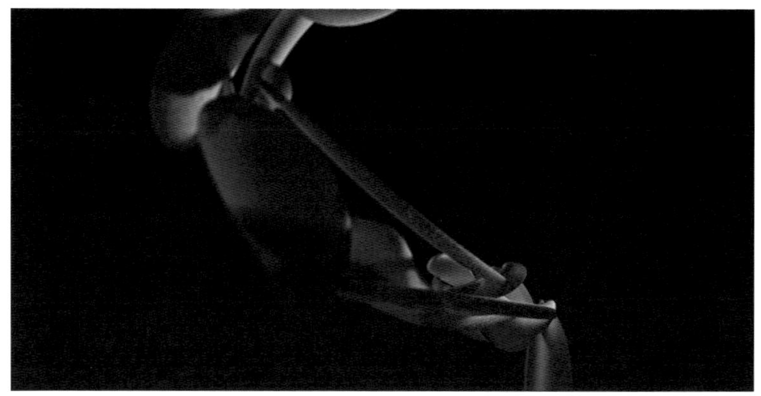

ABSTRACT 3
1006 x 505 pixels

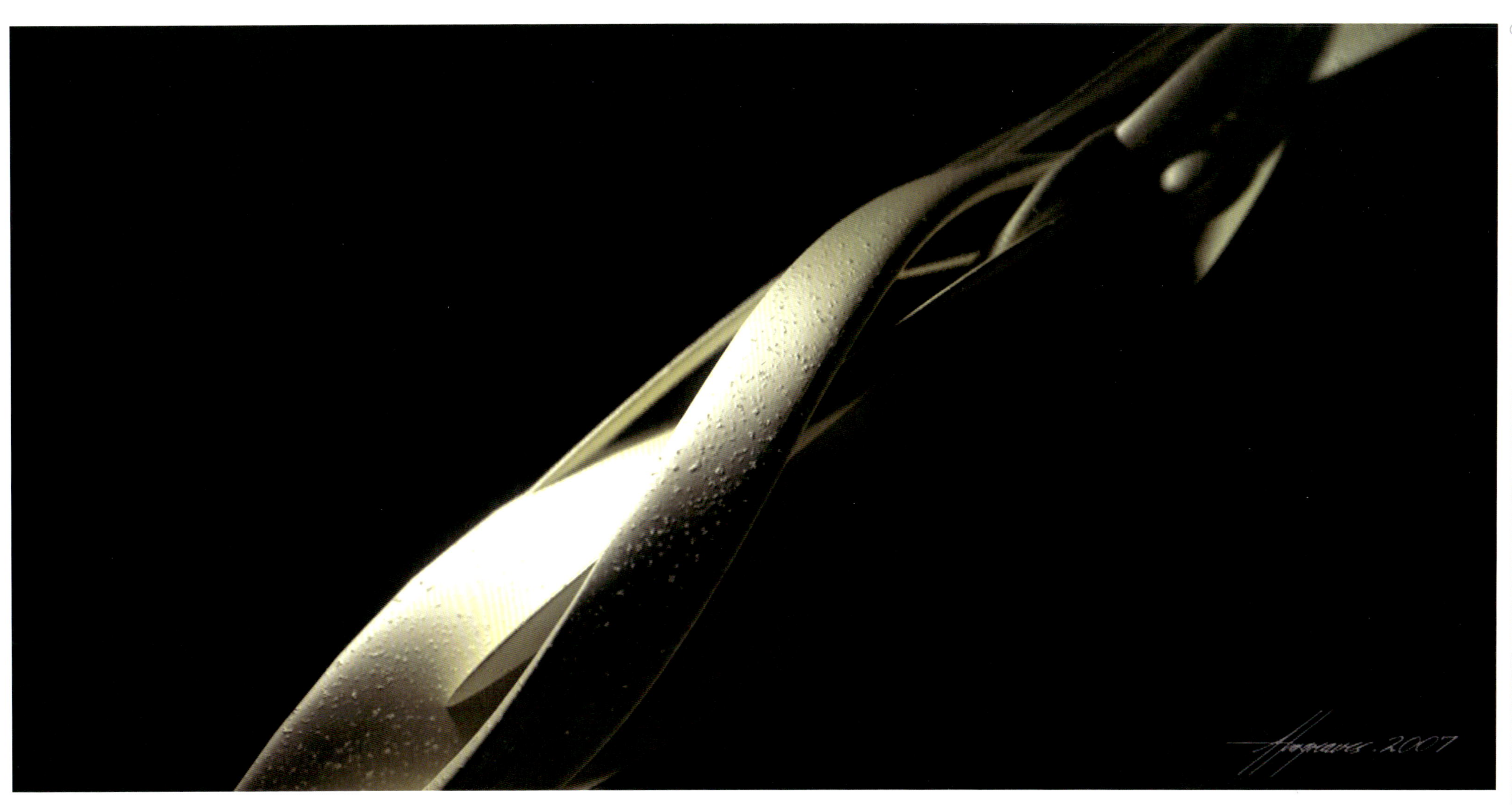

ABSTRACT 1

2400 x 1200 pixels

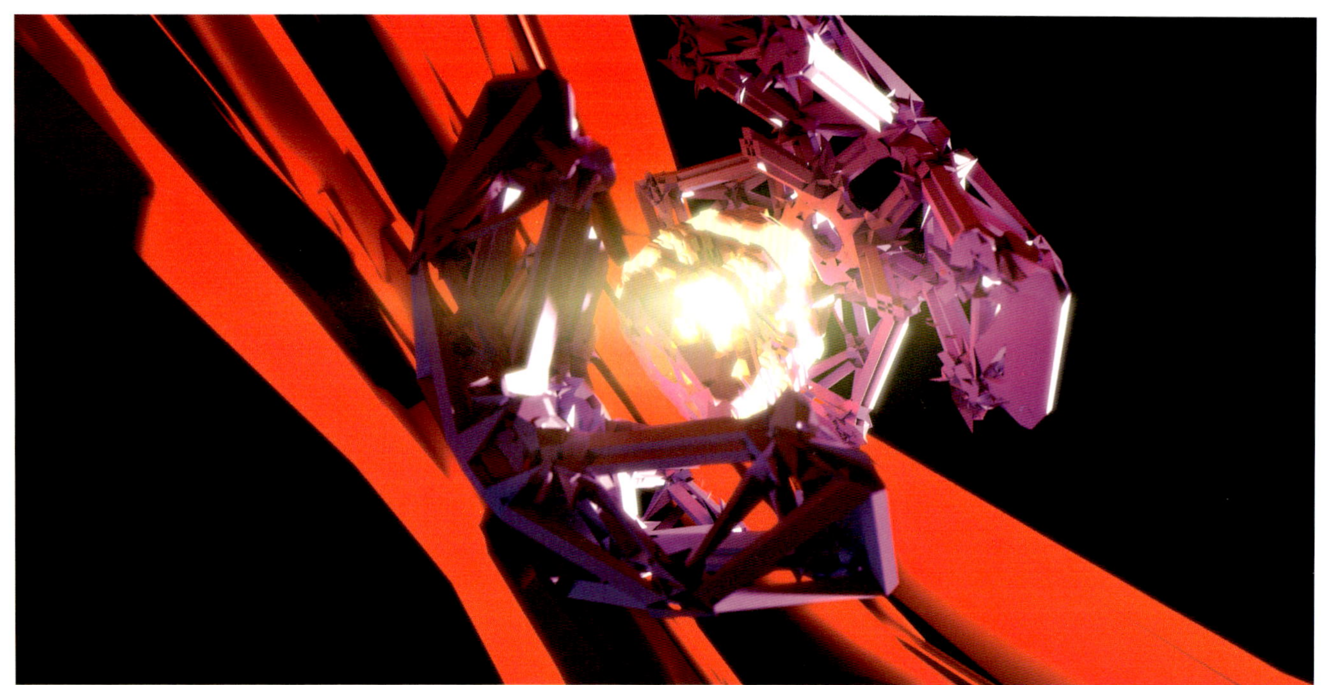

ABSTRACT 4
3000 x 1500 pixels

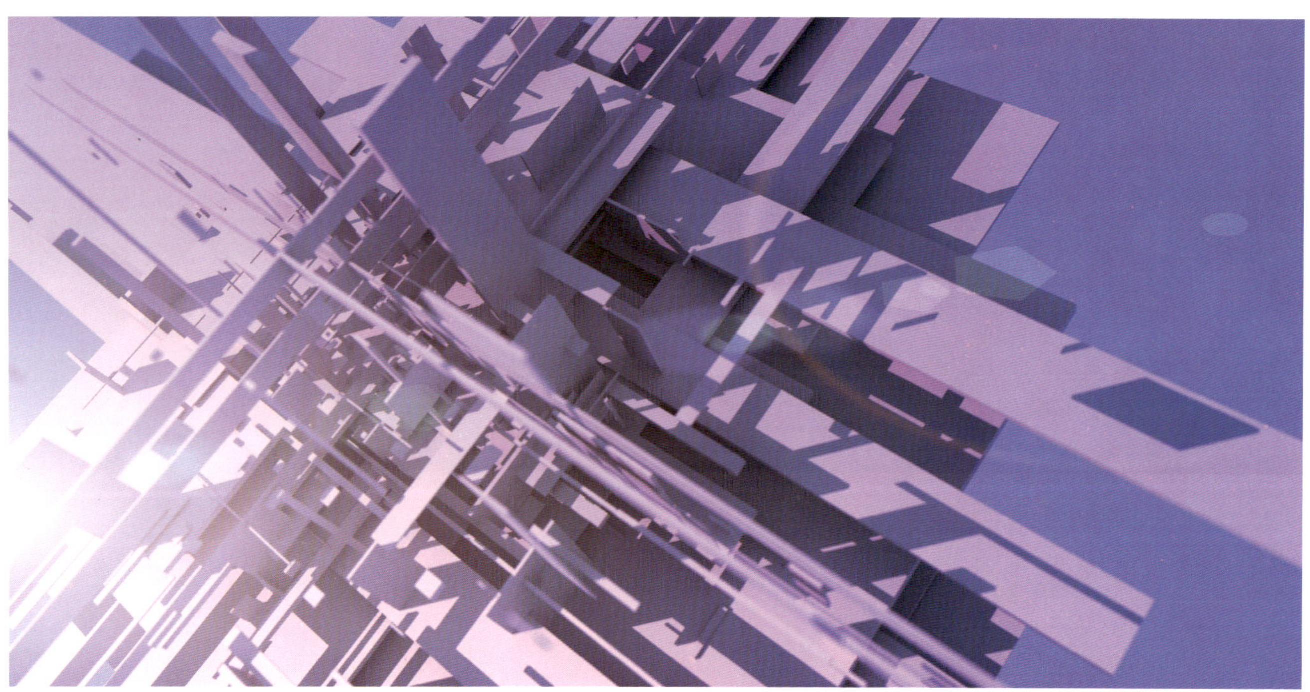

ABSTRACT 8
3000 x 1500 pixels

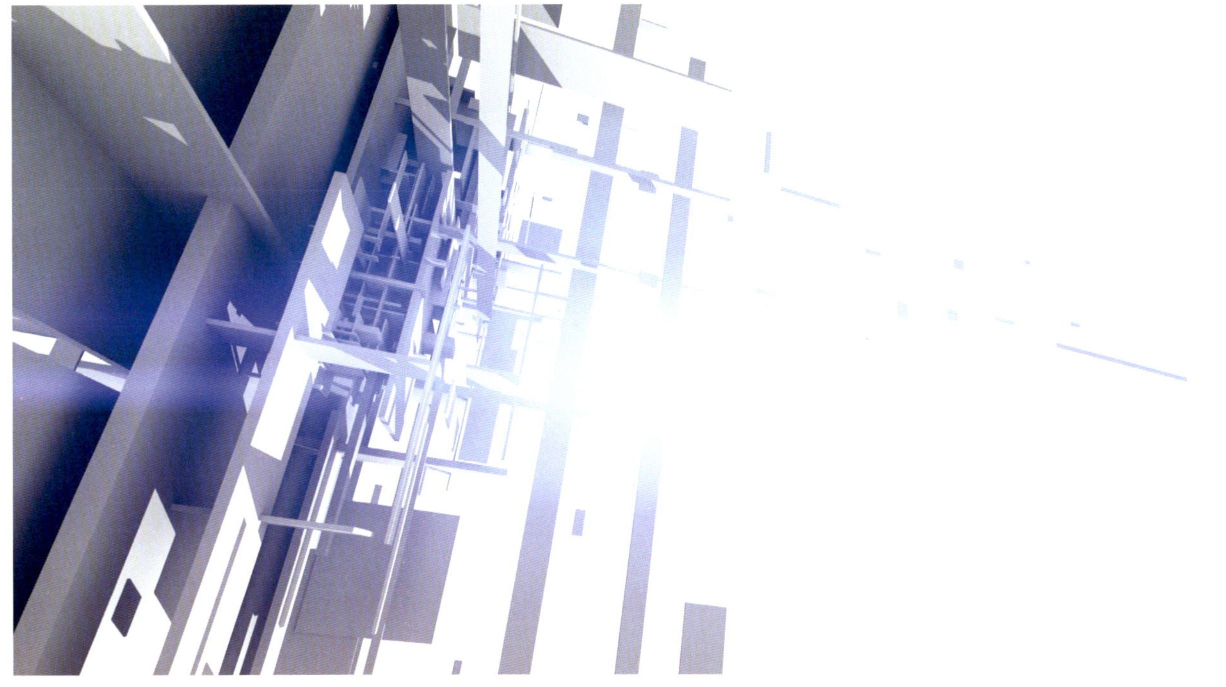

ABSTRACT 7
2000 x 1000 pixels

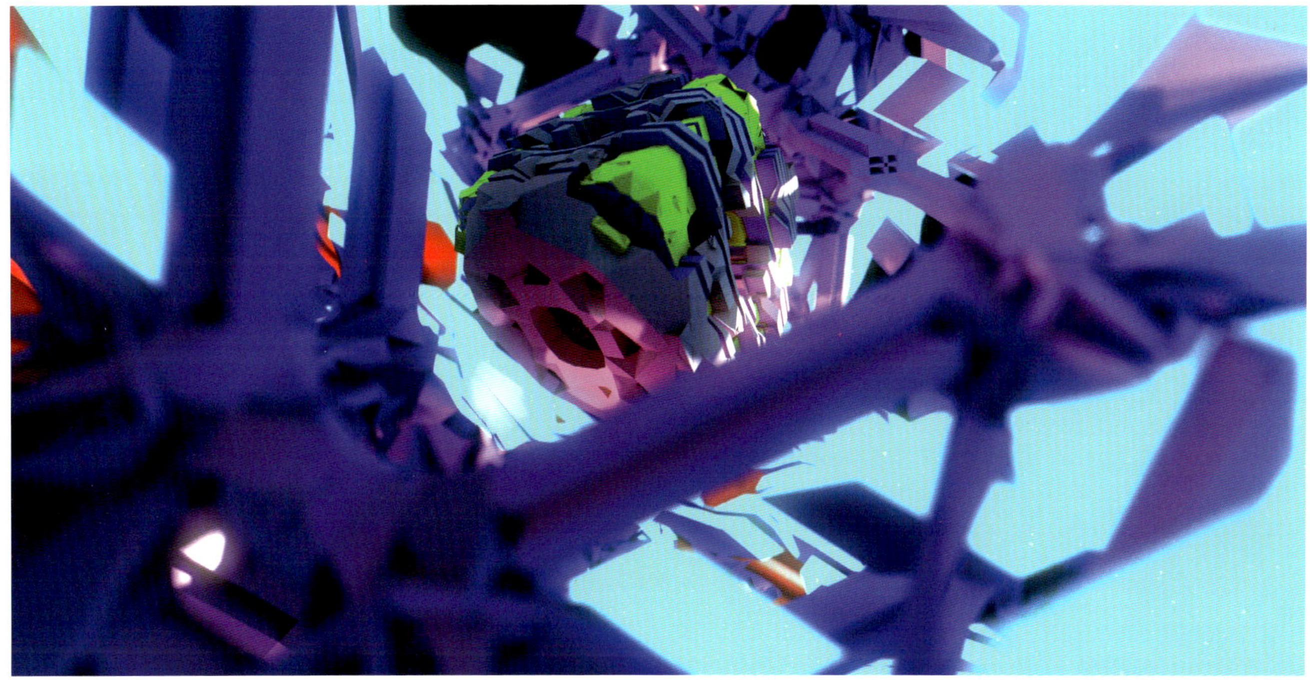

ABSTRACT 5
3000 x 1500 pixels

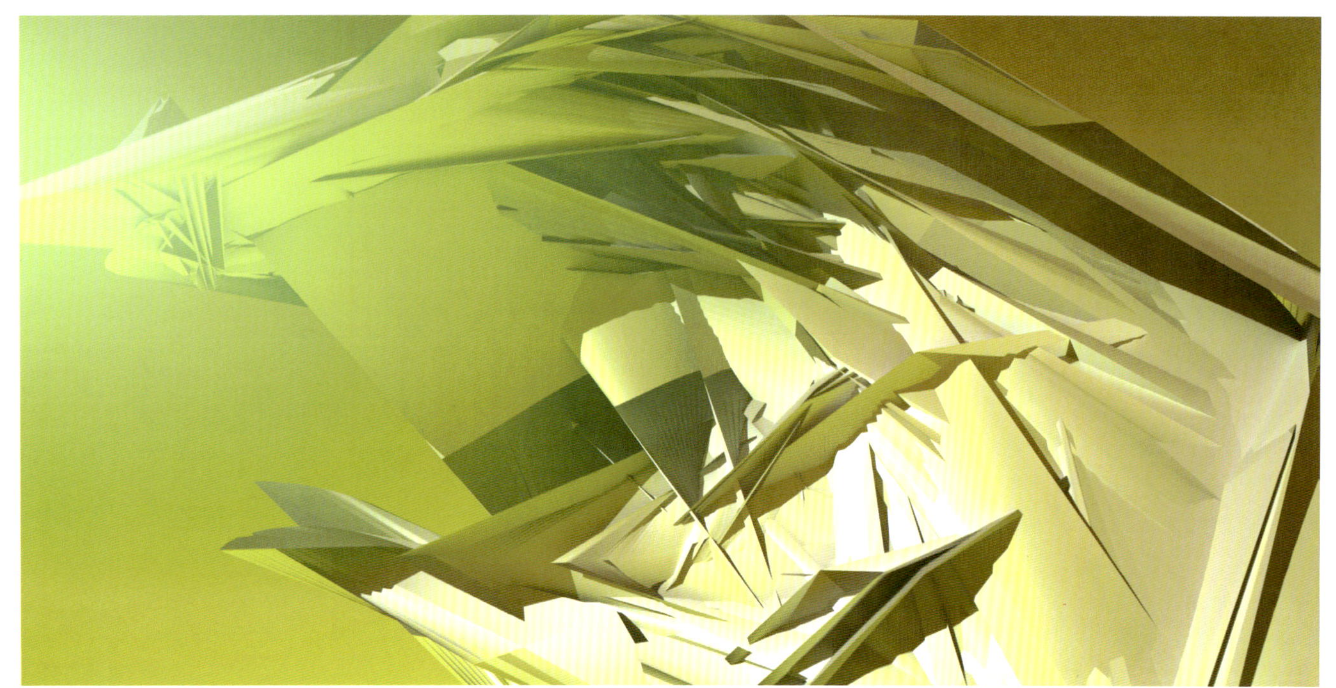

ABSTRACT 9
3000 x 1500 pixels

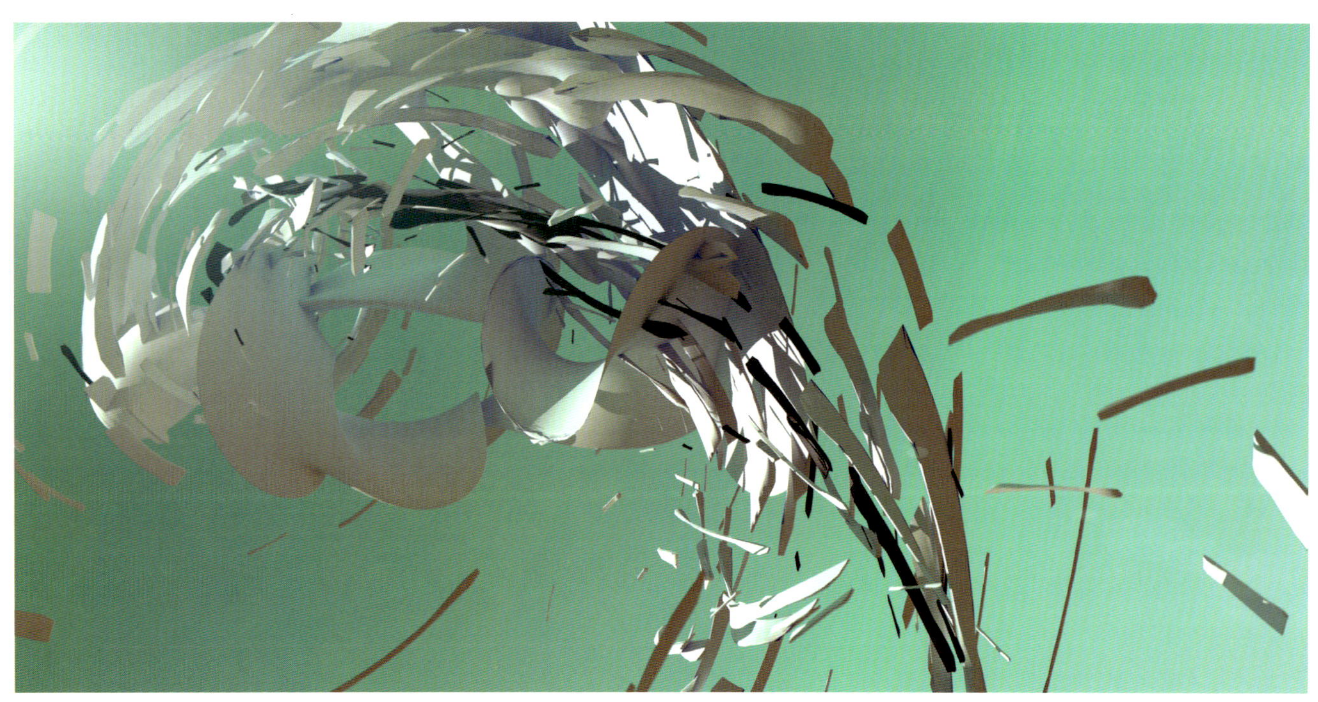

ABSTRACT 10
3000 x 1500 pixels

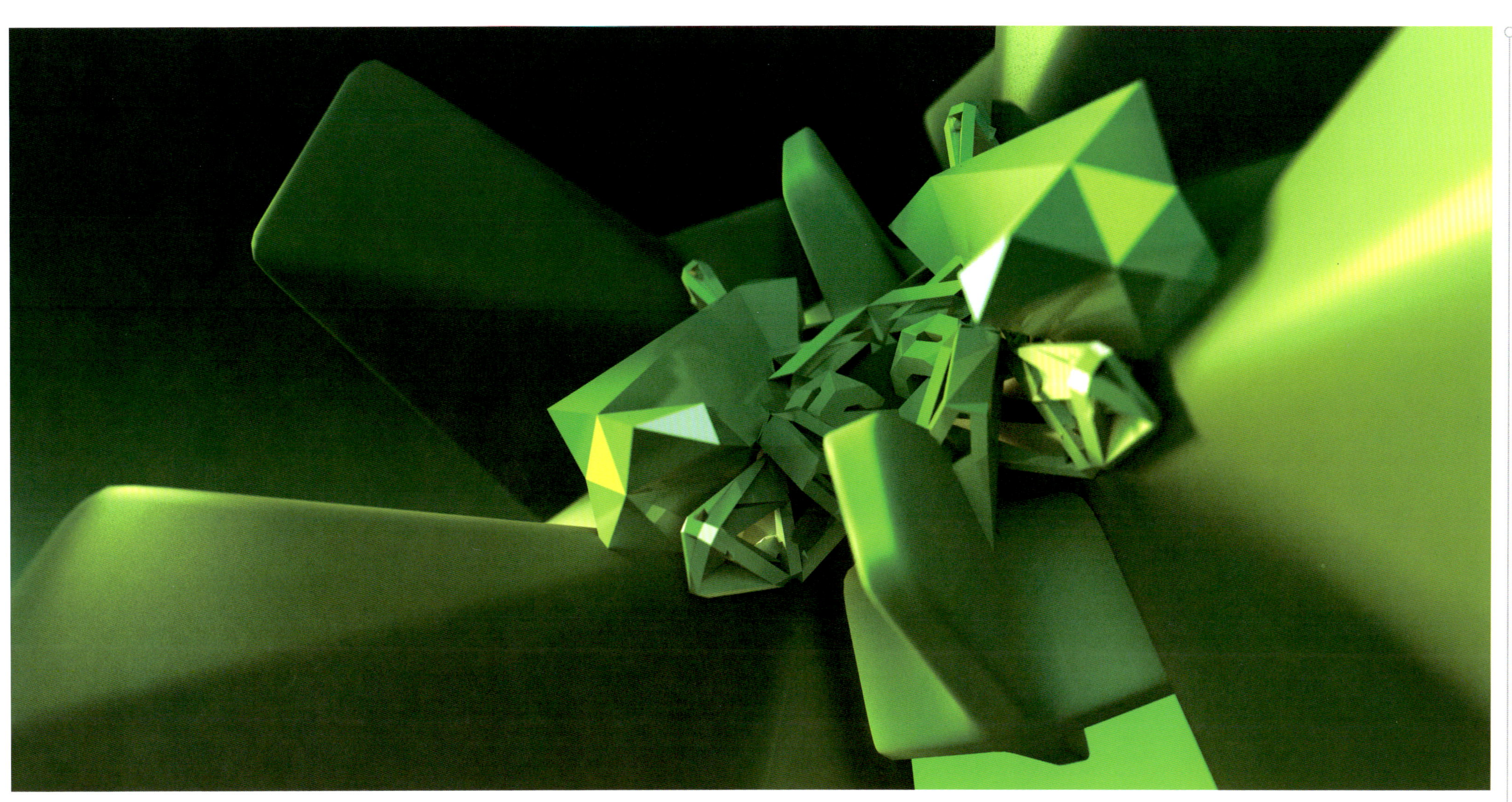

ABSTRACT 6
3000 x 1500 pixels

COMPUTERS

In 1980 I saw my first image of a supercomputer, the Cray-1 designed by the brilliant Seymour Cray. It was a beautiful design for the time, compact compared to previous supercomputers and very minimalist in its appearance. It had what looked like a set of seats surrounding the base, which contained the cooling units. Upon closer inspection, however, I discovered the image was actually a rendering of the Cray-1, not a photograph, and the rendering was done on the Cray. I was amazed at this. To me, at the time, it looked real.

Also around the same time I saw some digital flight simulations done by Evans and Sutherland, showing mountains, trees, houses, airports, bridges, etc. These simulations were all programmed on a supercomputer. All these images look somewhat crude today due to our advancement in technology, but these images were the seeds of what I wanted to do, and eventually explore.

In the late 1990s, prior to my involvement at Industrial Light & Magic, I was hired at Pixar as a visualist. It was there that I met Steve Jobs, whose book about his and Steve Wozniak's invention of the Macintosh fueled my interest in the future of what I call our second brain, the computer. At Pixar it was incredible what they were doing, and being surrounded by the talent there certainly rubbed off on me. It was wonderful to do designs and then have them built in the computer in 3D, to see them rotated, and to move in and around them.

In the application of design, computers have become incredibly valuable assets. To me, the computer is but another way one can express his or her creativity. I don't consider it as a substitute for a sketch or a painting—it is but another tool.

I feel a great privilege to be alive in this digital era. To be a part of and to contribute to the awareness of the possibilities of what the computer can offer us, is something not to be taken for granted.

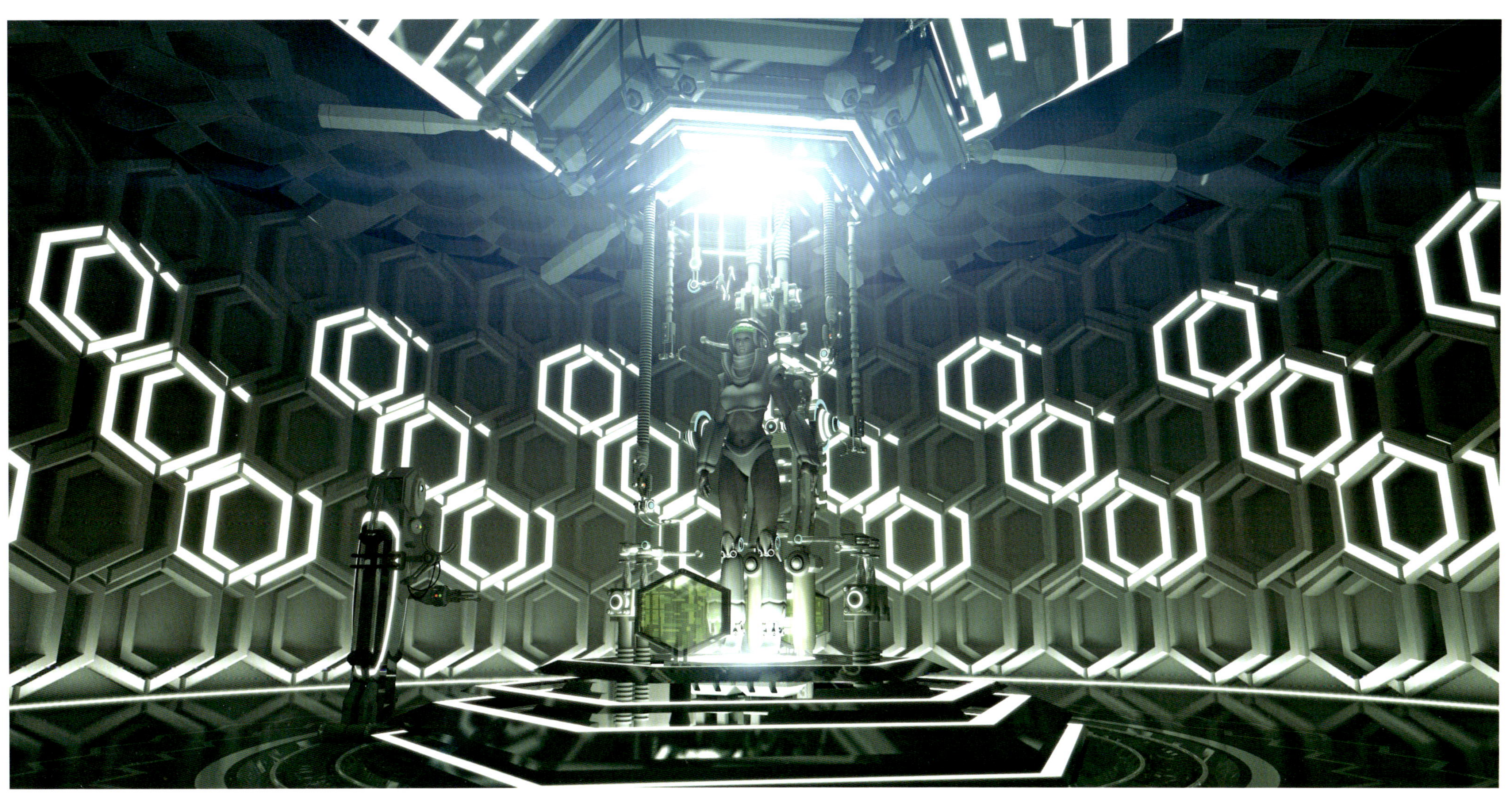

03
CONCENTRIC DIAPHUM
3000 x 1500 pixels
SEÁN HARGREAVES : PLACES

04

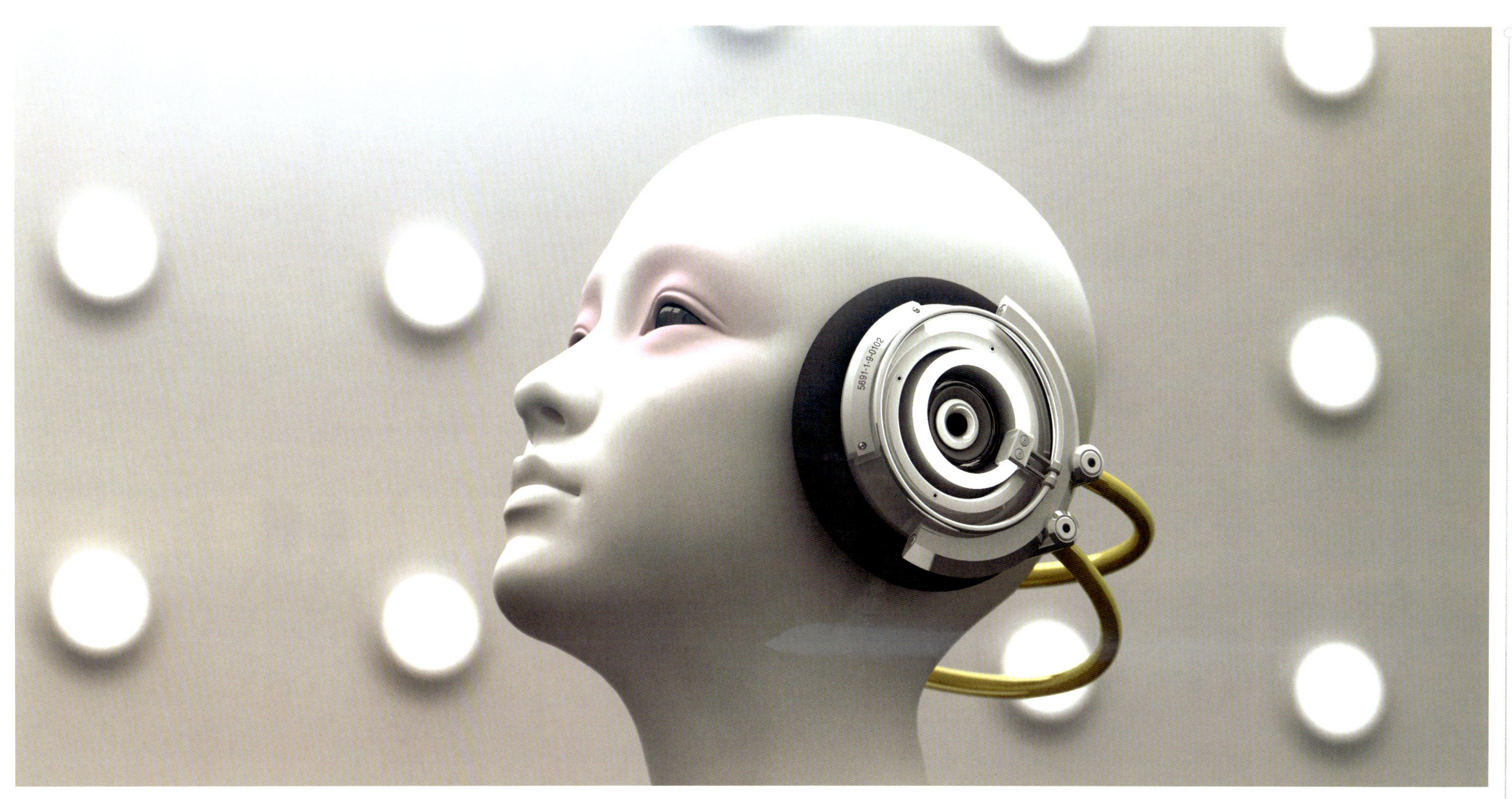

4 FOUR
3000 x 1500 pixels

05

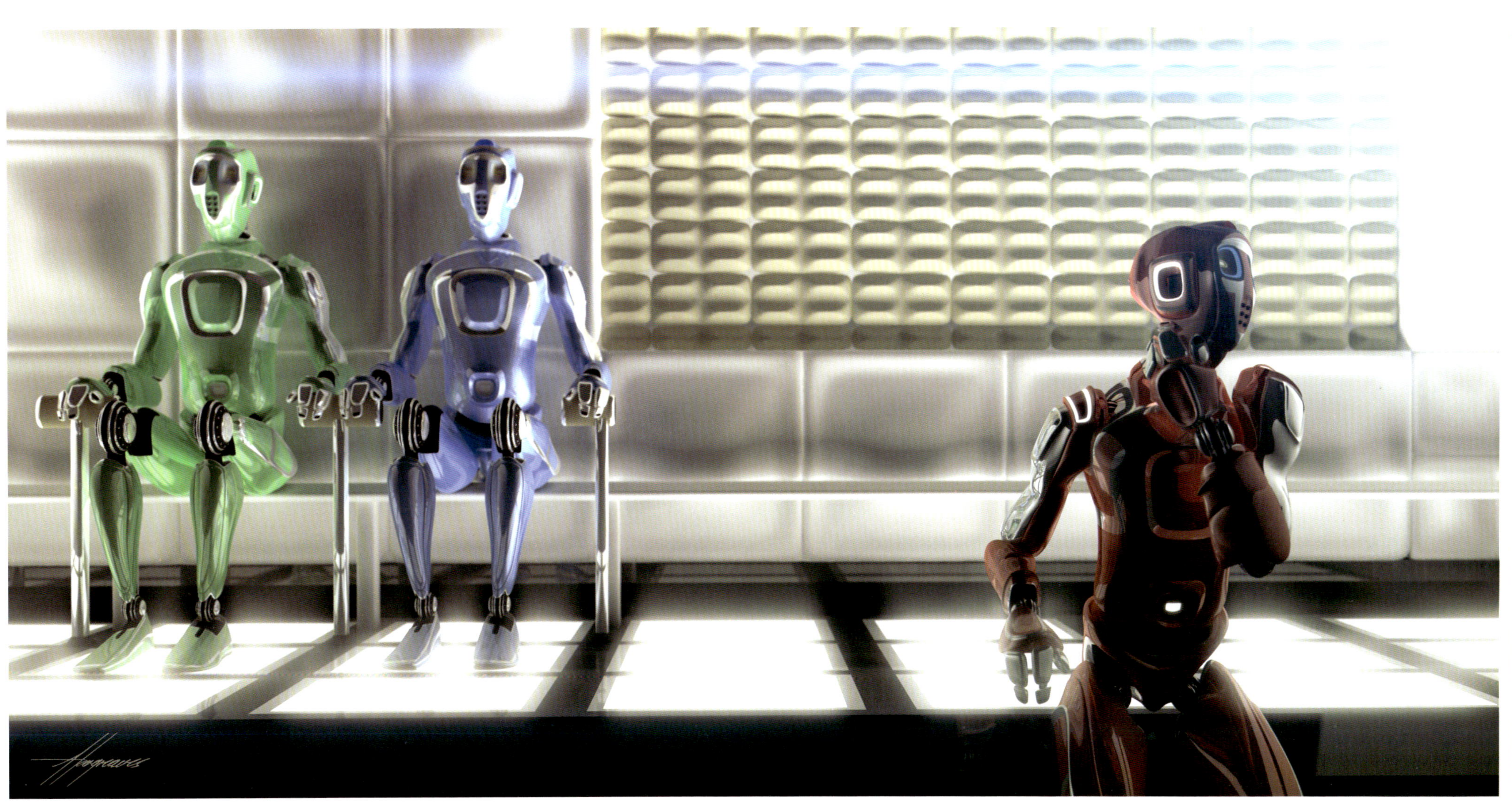

ROOM 45
3000 x 1500 pixels

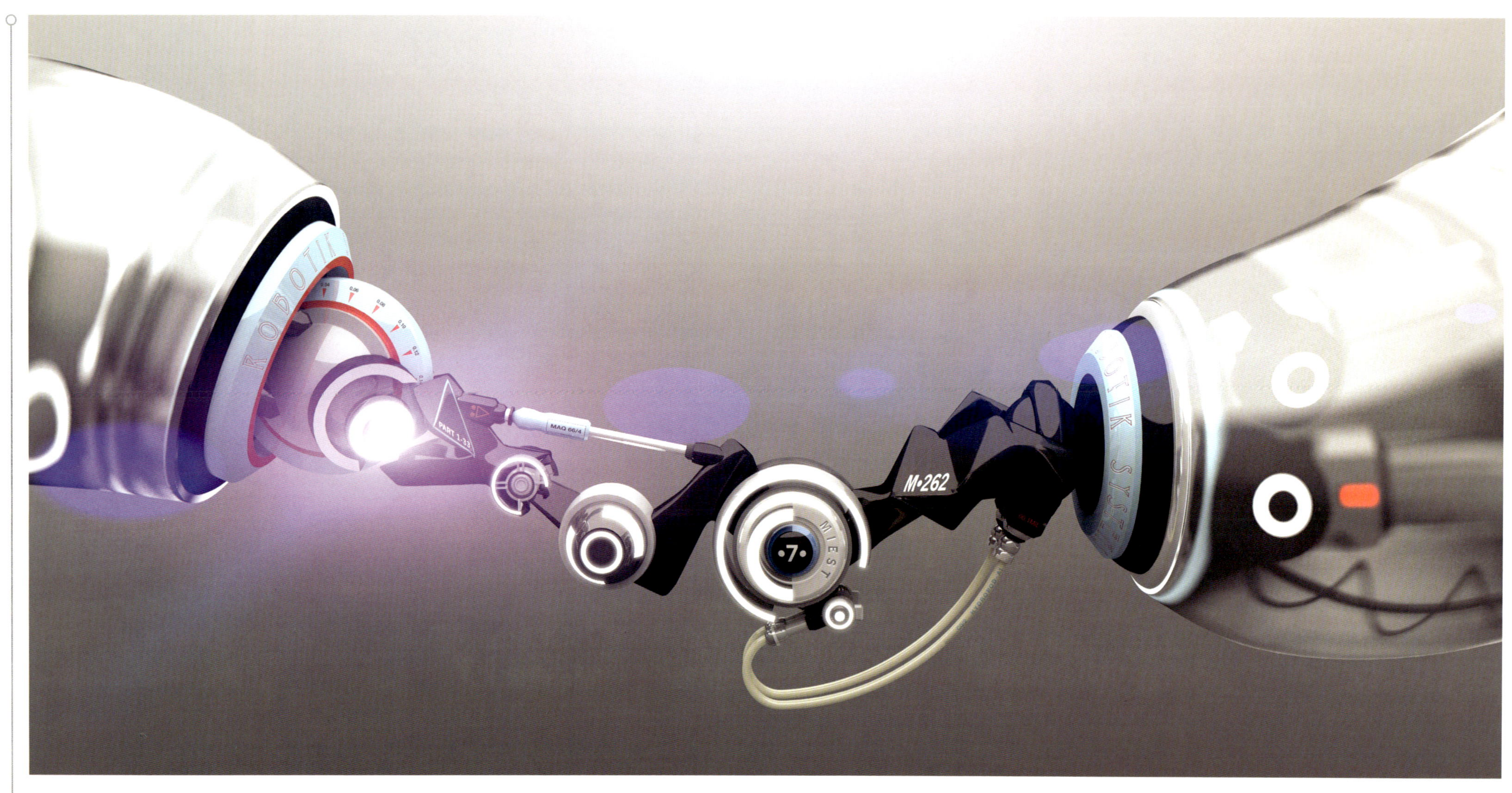

DIAMETRICAL BELCATARKUM
3000 x 1500 pixels

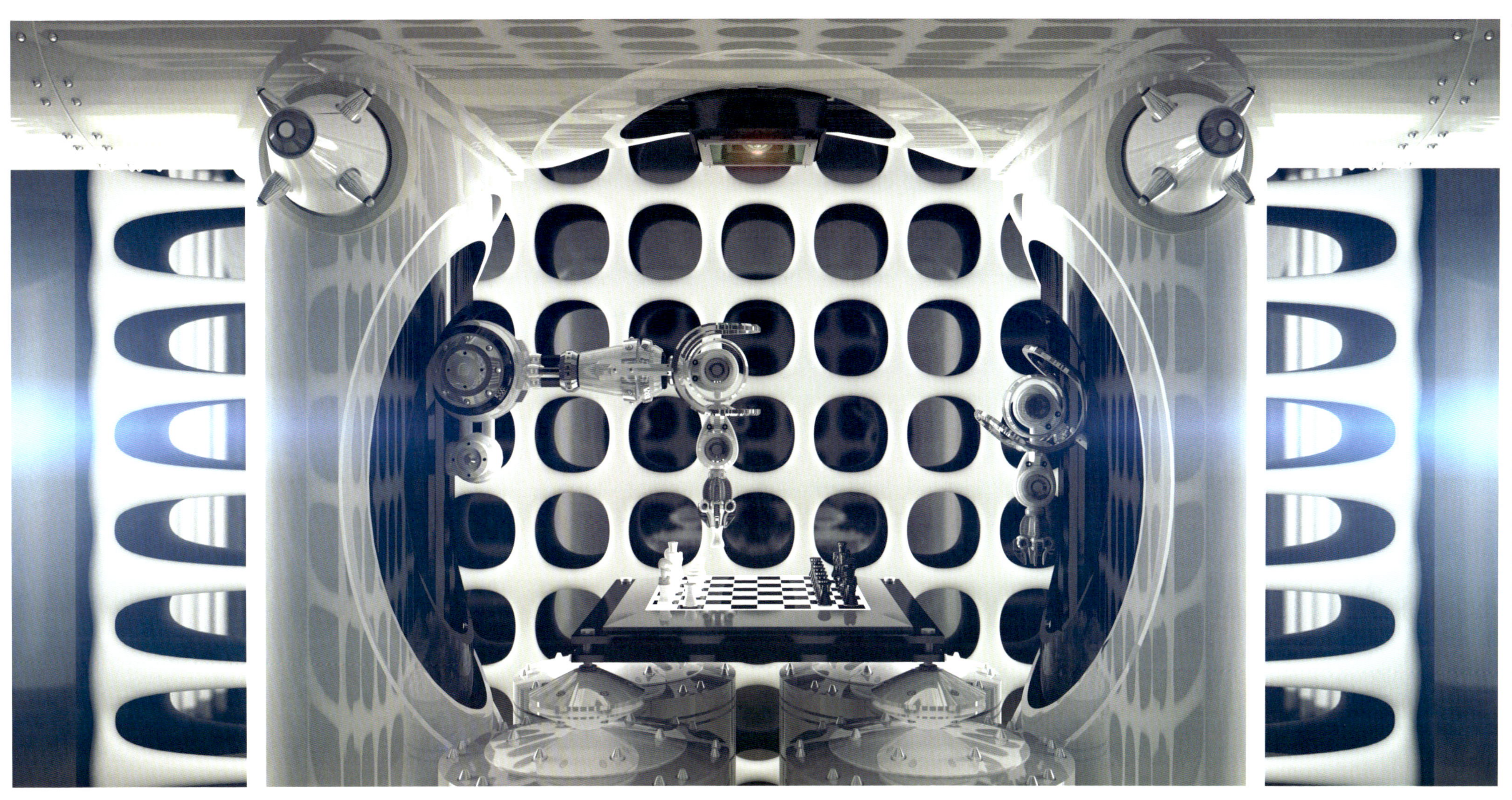

07

VEHICLES

Why do all cars look alike?

The problem is quite simple: packaging. A car is like a T-shirt, because of the packaging requirement you can only do so much with the design. A car designer has to tend with the engine size, storage size, and passenger count. These are the basic requirements that determine the vehicle shape. Sometimes it seems no matter what car you originally draw, once it goes through the required filters, it's just not the same, so as a designer one must concentrate on the subtle details inside and out, and shifts in body shape, and that's what will set the design apart.

I worked for General Motors Advanced Concepts Center in Newbury Park, California. I saw some amazing designs there. Around the offices were beautiful starship paintings by John Berkey, and it was really inspiring to work there. It's not easy to project the design of a car, or to sell a particular car as a need. We were given a project of our own choosing; I chose to work on the design of an inexpensive one-person car for third-world countries, kind of like a motorized rickshaw. It was developed from the pod cars I had been sketching at Art Center, and would run from an electric motor. Such design studies are crucial, I believe, to understanding problems and issues that go beyond the mere aesthetic of a product.

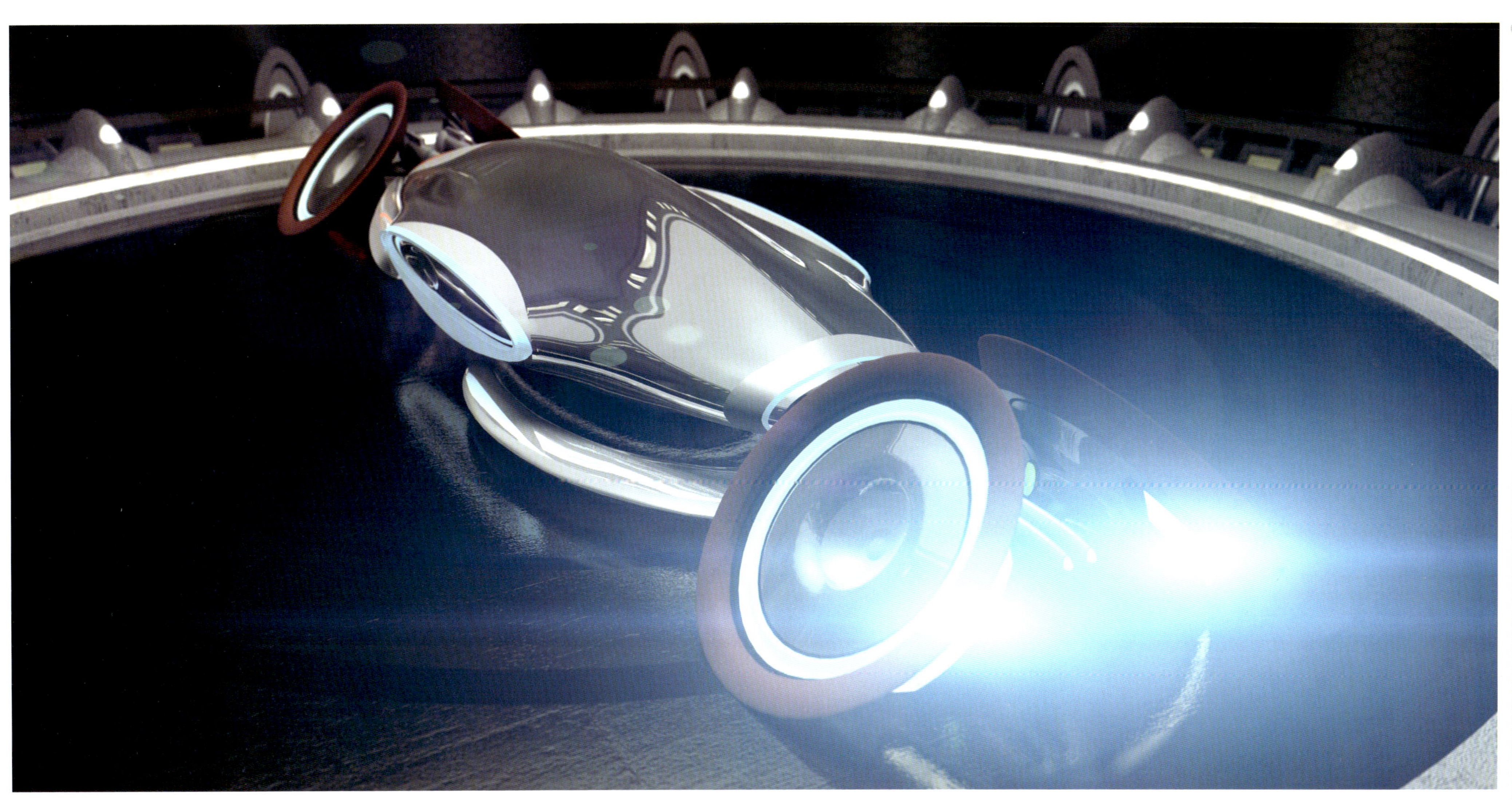

08

TRAVELLER
4000 x 2000 pixels

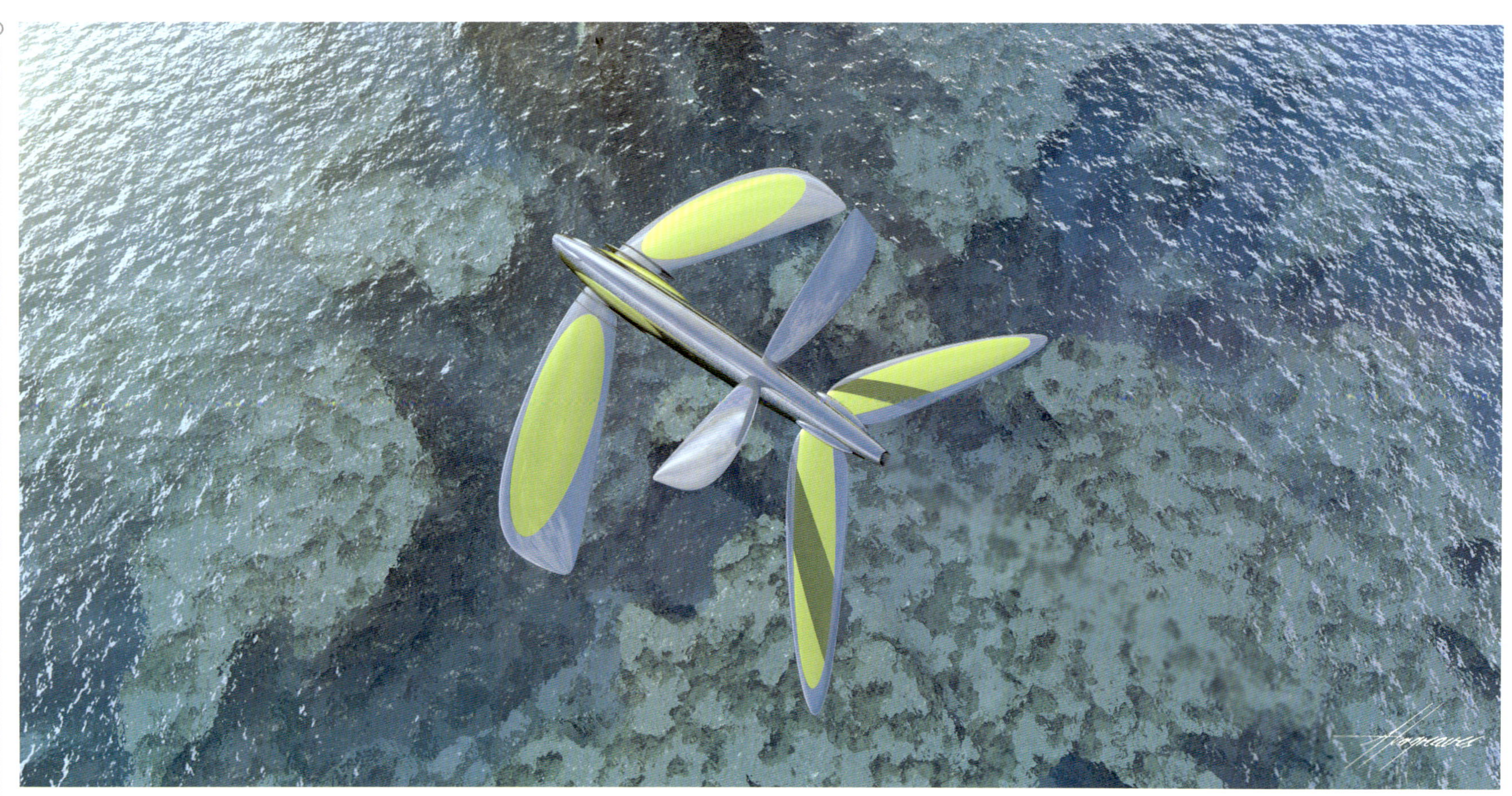

09
PINNACLES
2000 x 1000 pixels

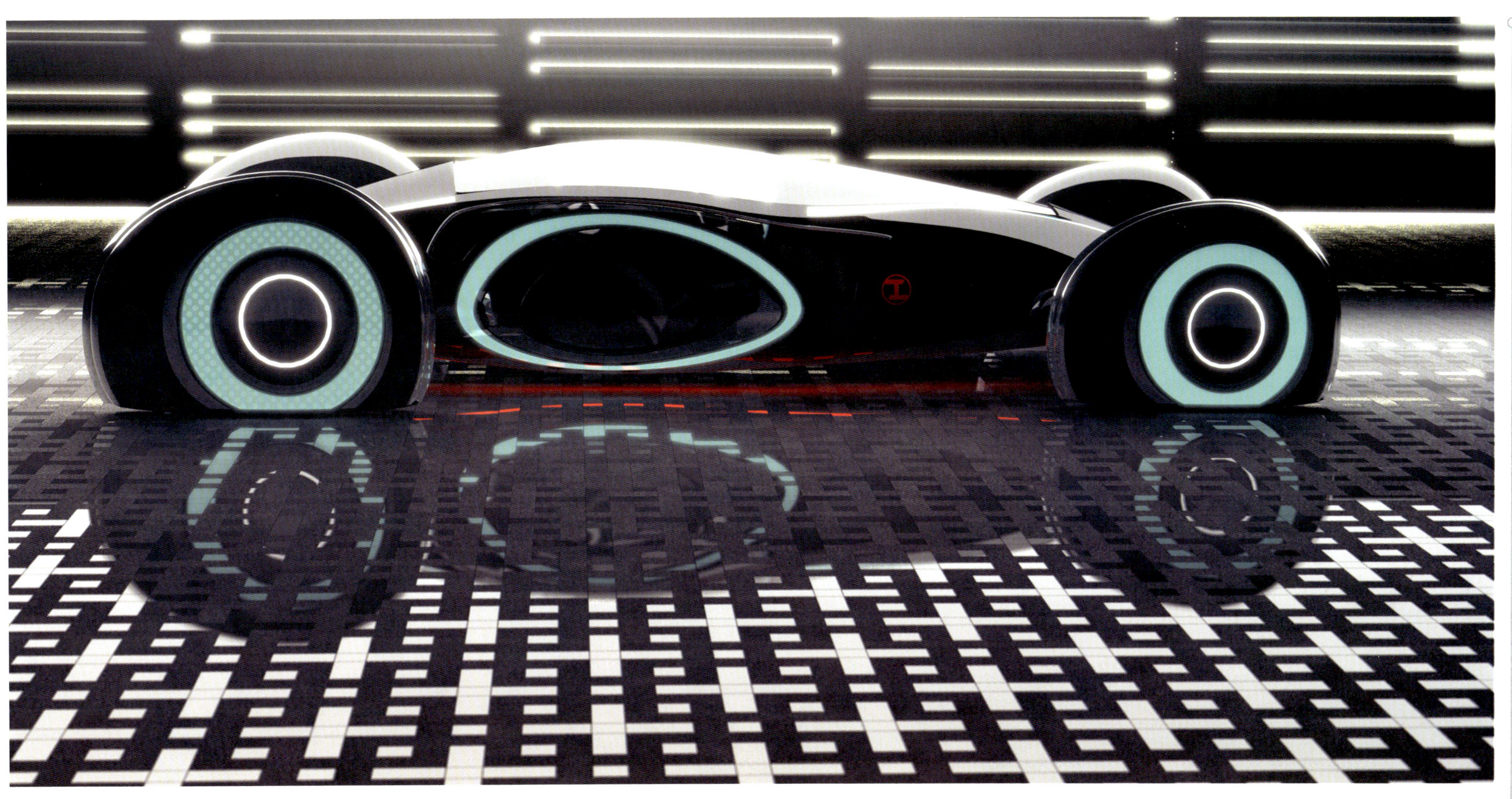

THE BEGINNING
3000 x 1500 pixels

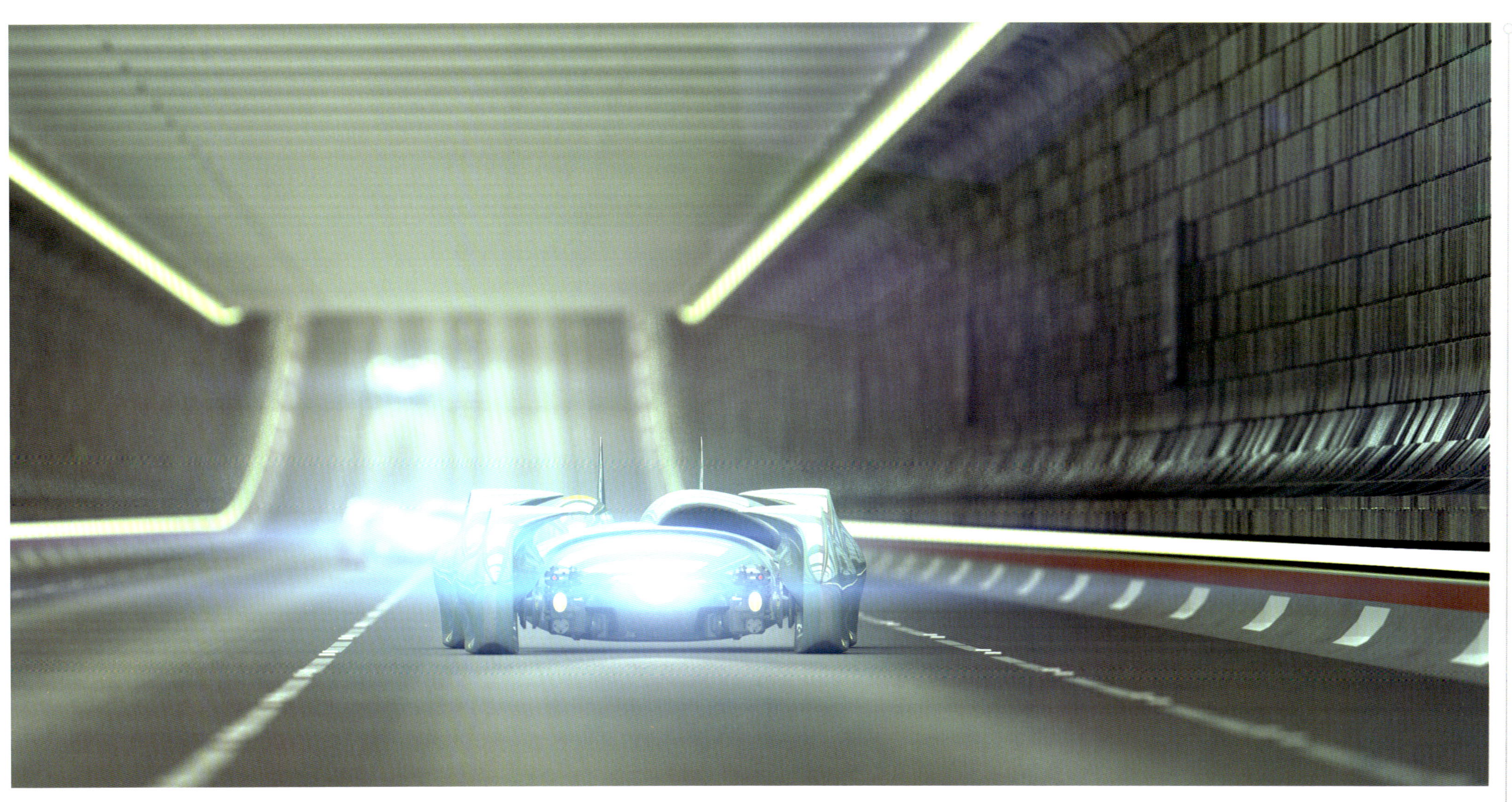

⟨ 1 . 1 . 1 ⟩
3000 x 1500 pixels

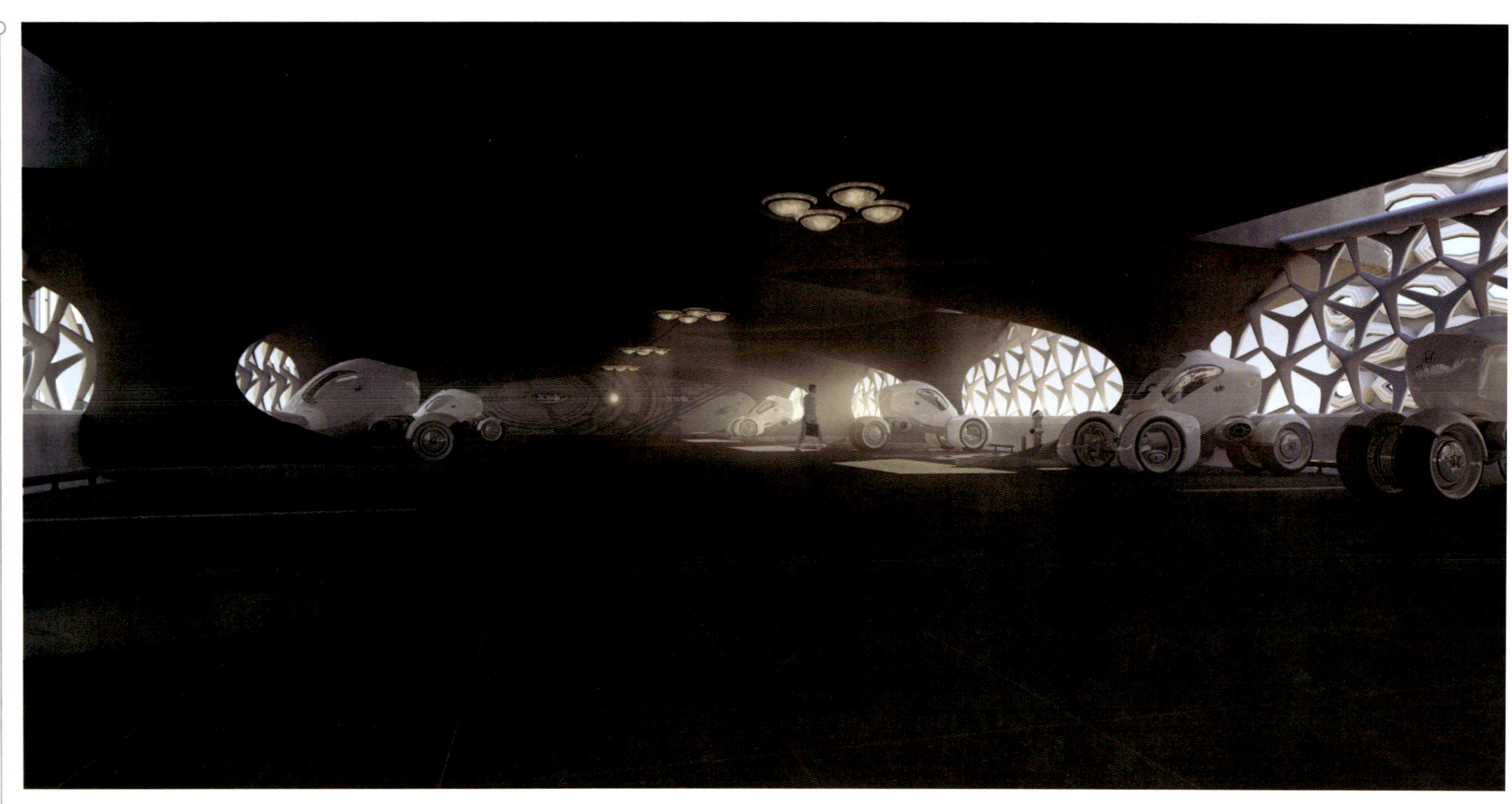

SO MUCH FOR THAT
2000 x 1000 pixels

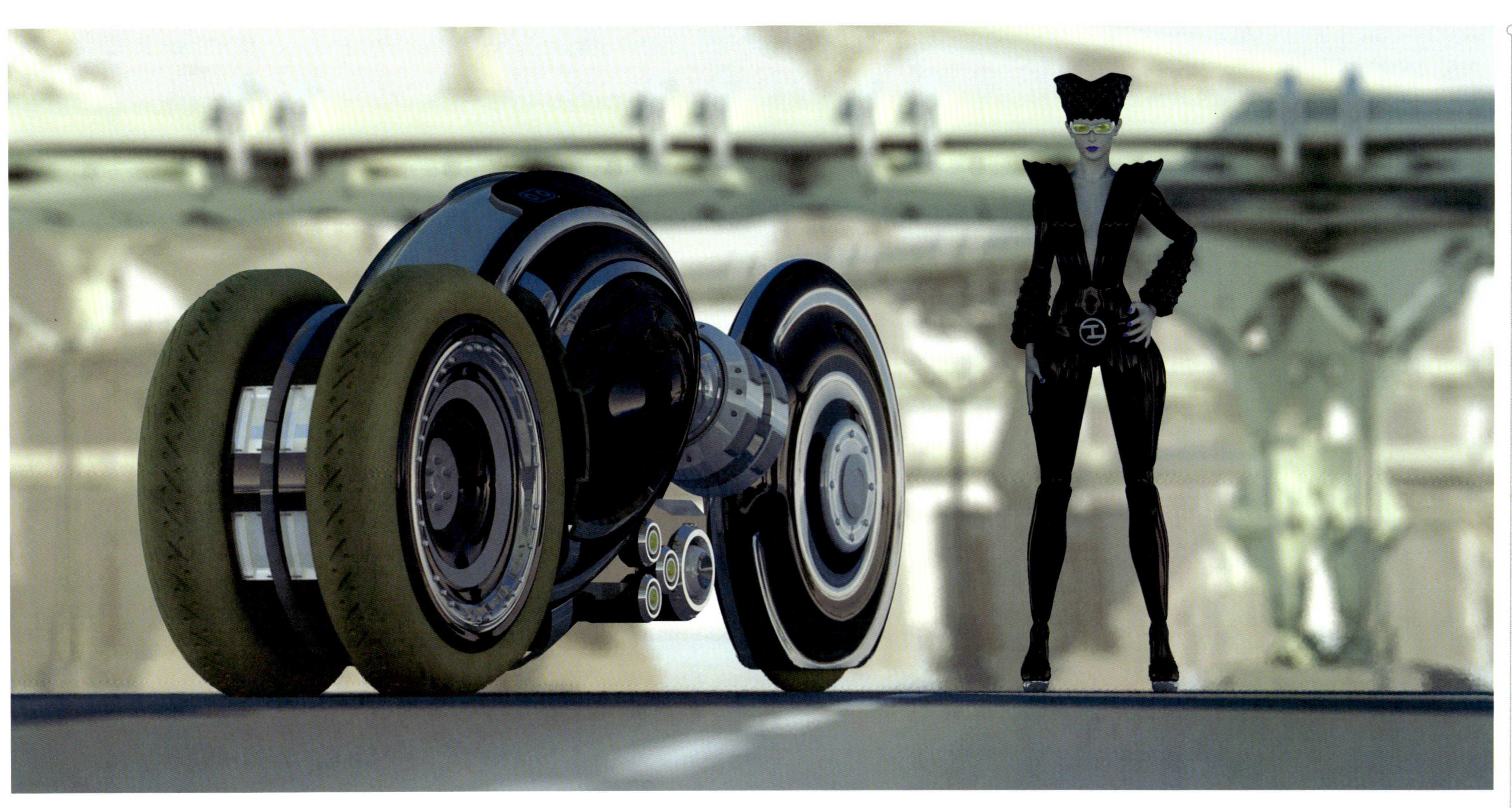

13
SHEN TANTREMO
3000 x 1500 pixels

74

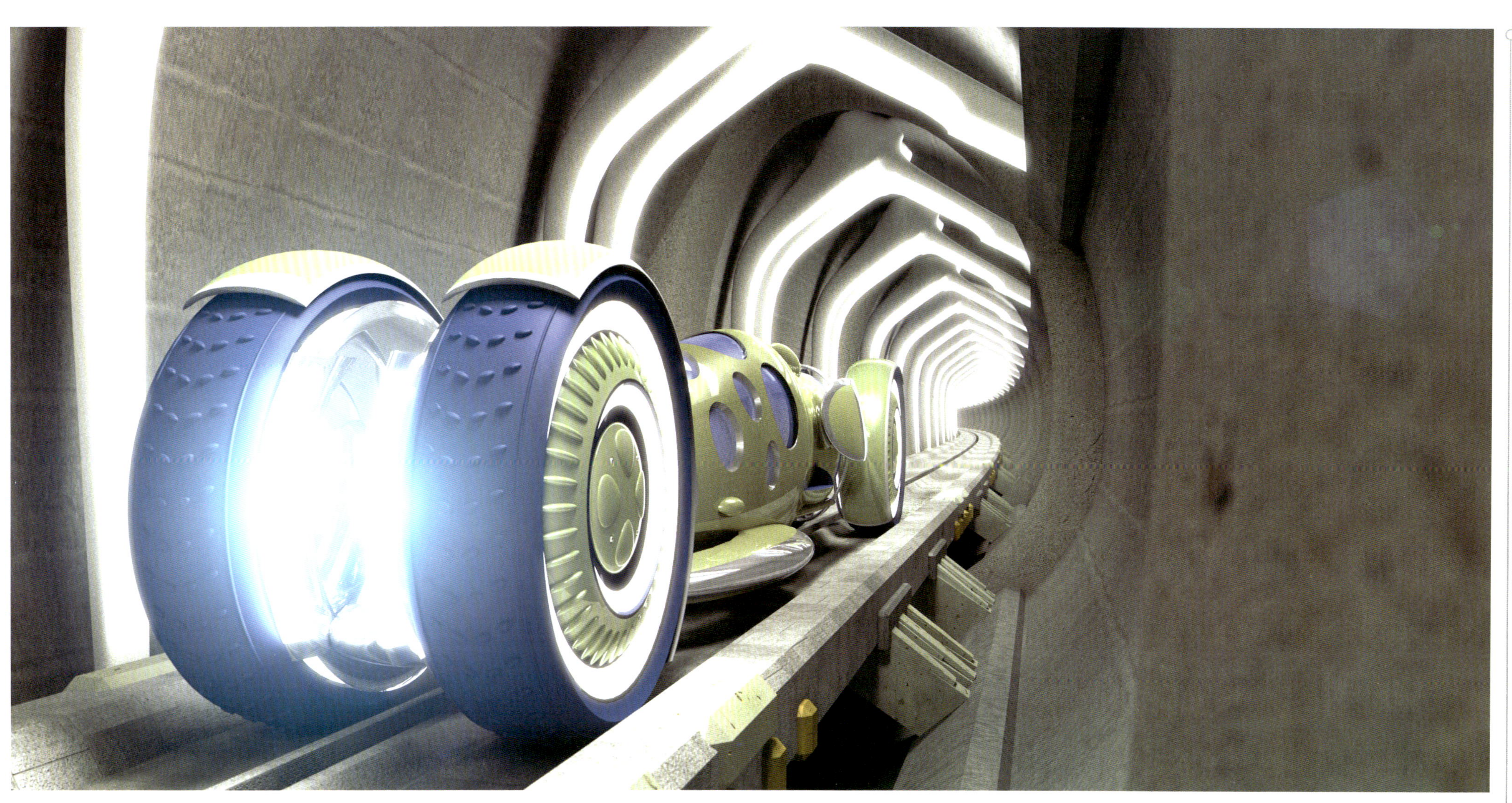
A > B
3000 x 1500 pixels

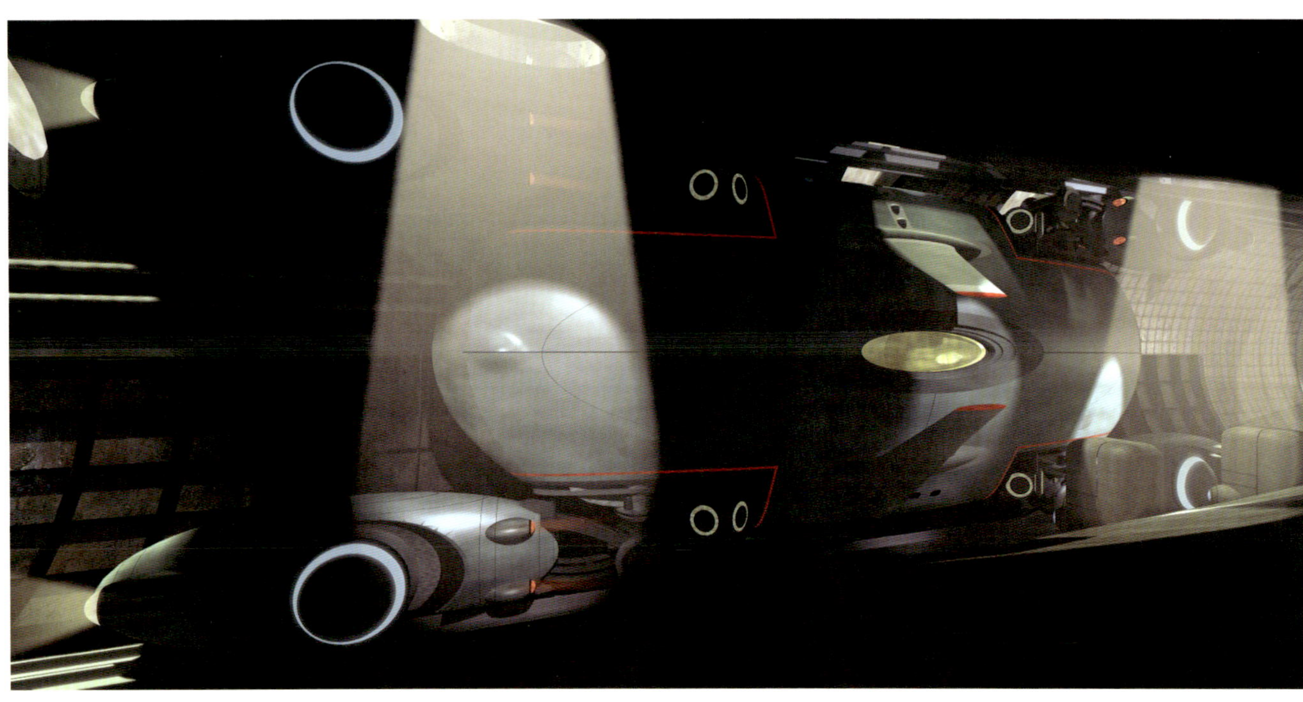

15

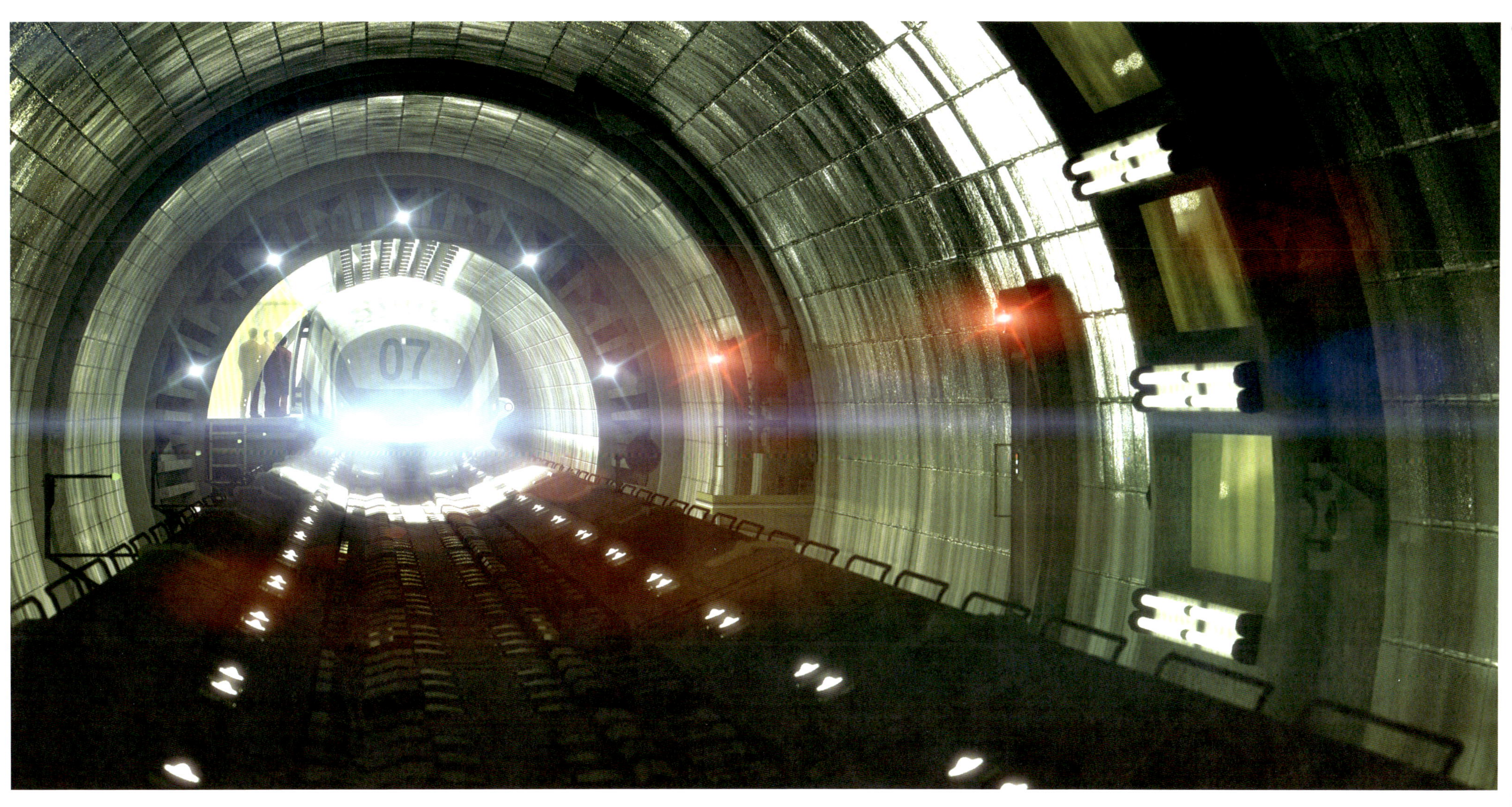

16

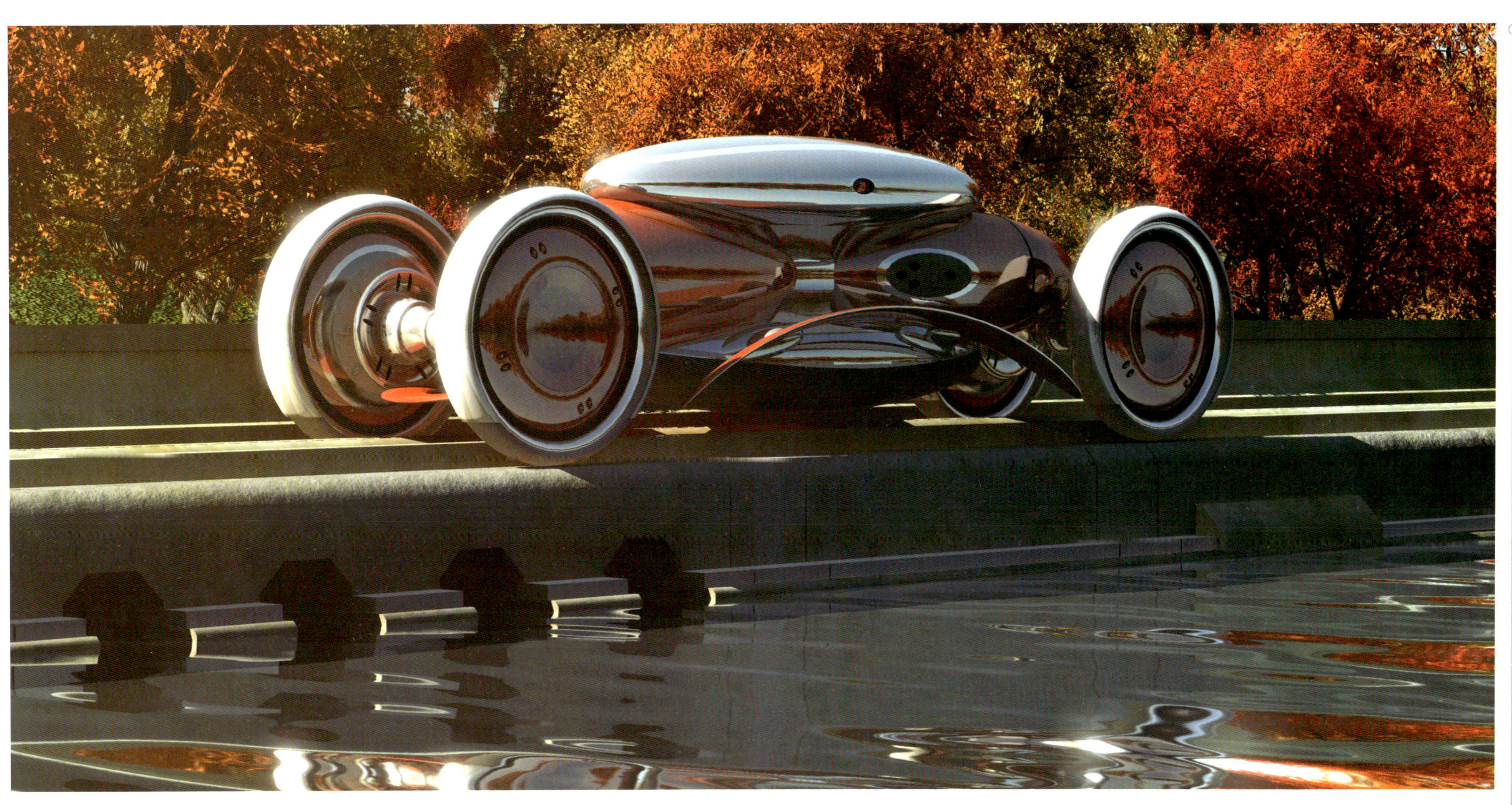

PLENB CROSSING
3000 x 1500 pixels

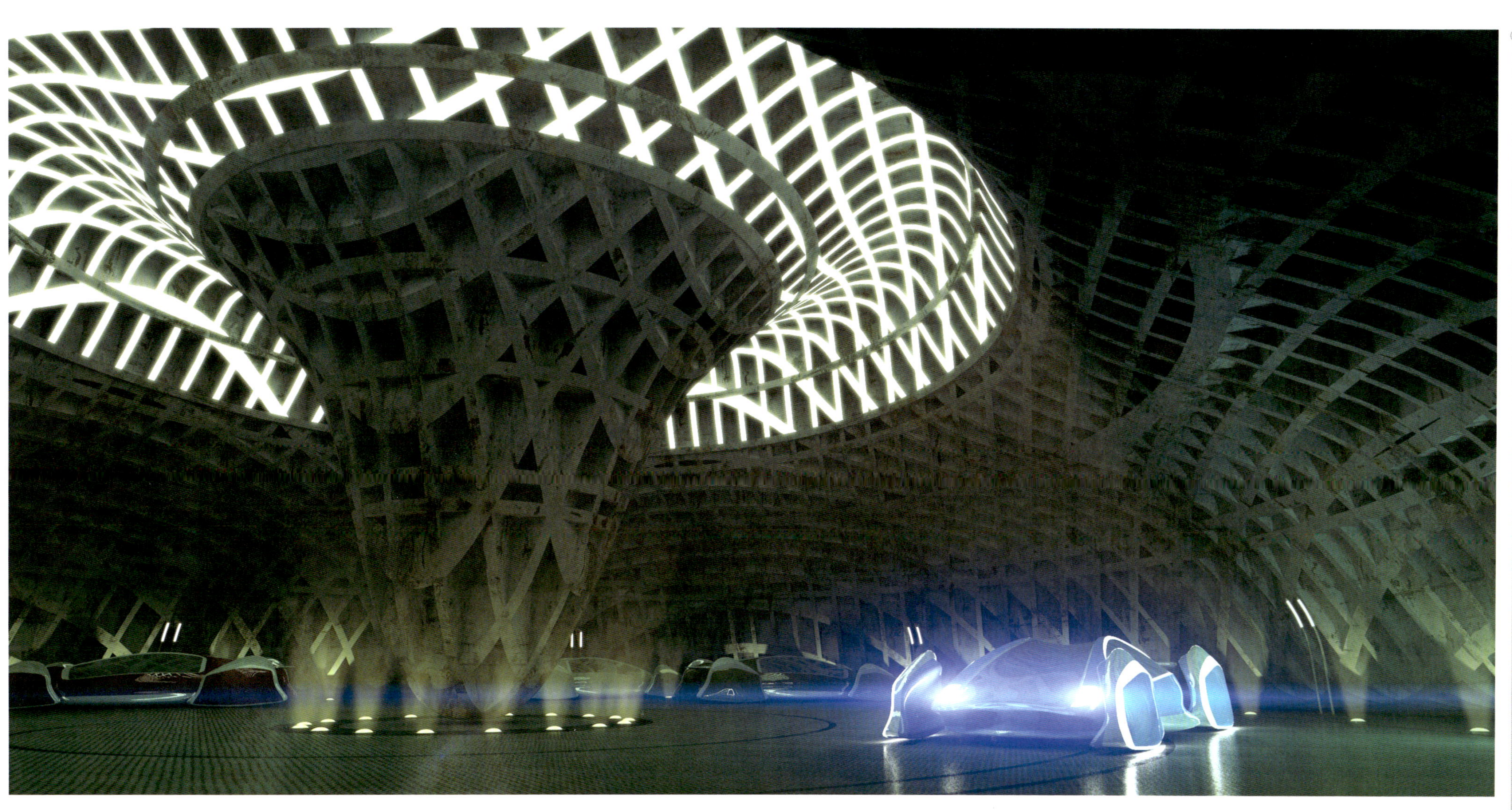

FRAME
3000 x 1500 pixels

ARCHITECTURE

In recent years, thanks to the digital medium, architects have pushed the boundaries of structure and engineering, and many new building shapes have emerged. Modern architects and designers have re-invented the art of decoration and introduced new shapes and graphics, while at the same time using well-known materials in different ways.

Living in Paris I was subjected to different types of architecture. It was during this time I studied to a great degree the proportion and visual weight of buildings. I remember numerous days walking around and sketching buildings and details, sometimes enhancing or redesigning them.

Architecture is a very complex medium. The flow of people through spaces is an art unto itself. It's very easy to overdesign or undersign a space. In some minimalist rooms the smallest detail can make a huge difference. In some heavily ornate rooms nothing is left untouched, and the space becomes almost a sculpture unto itself.

Some of the most mundane places can be visually interesting. Take a parking structure, for example. In the 1960s here in Los Angeles, it seems that parking structures were given a much larger respect than now, and some of the ceiling details are incredible. It's easy to drive into a parking space and get out and walk straight to an elevator without seeing the space you're in. Next time just sit there for a moment... take a look around.

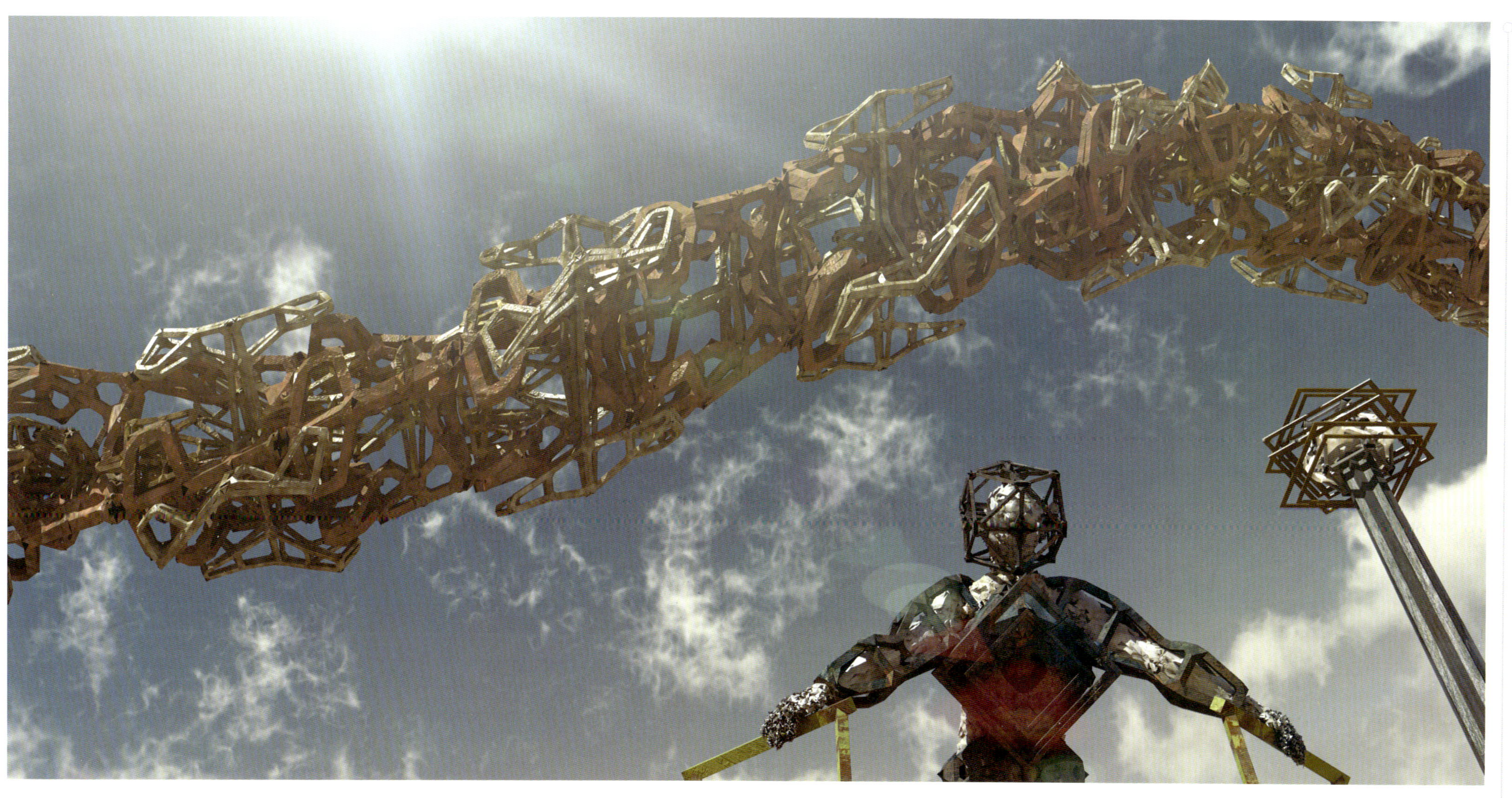
19
AERIAL SPINE
3000 x 1500 pixels

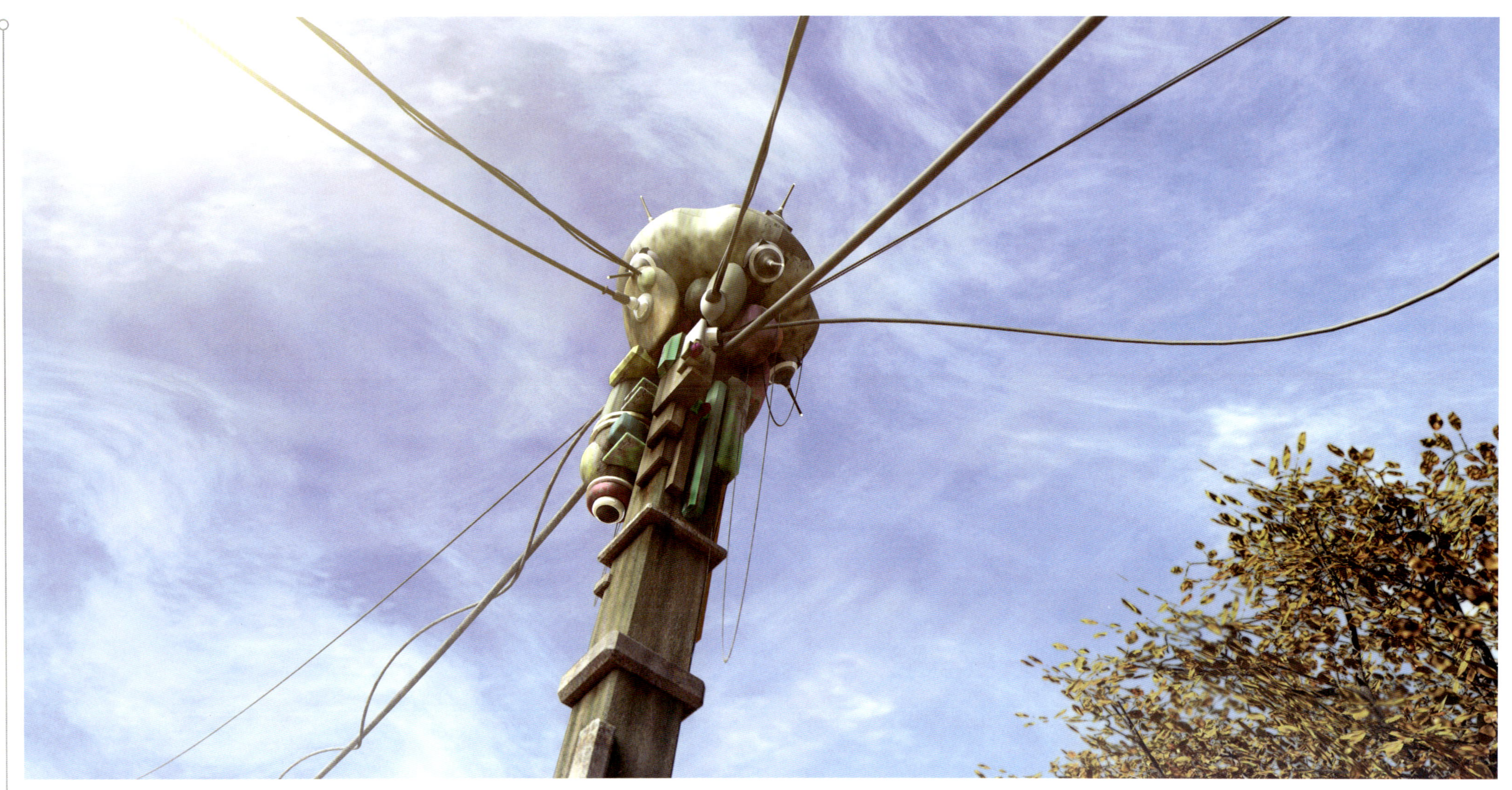

ELECTRICAL POLE
6000 x 3000 pixels

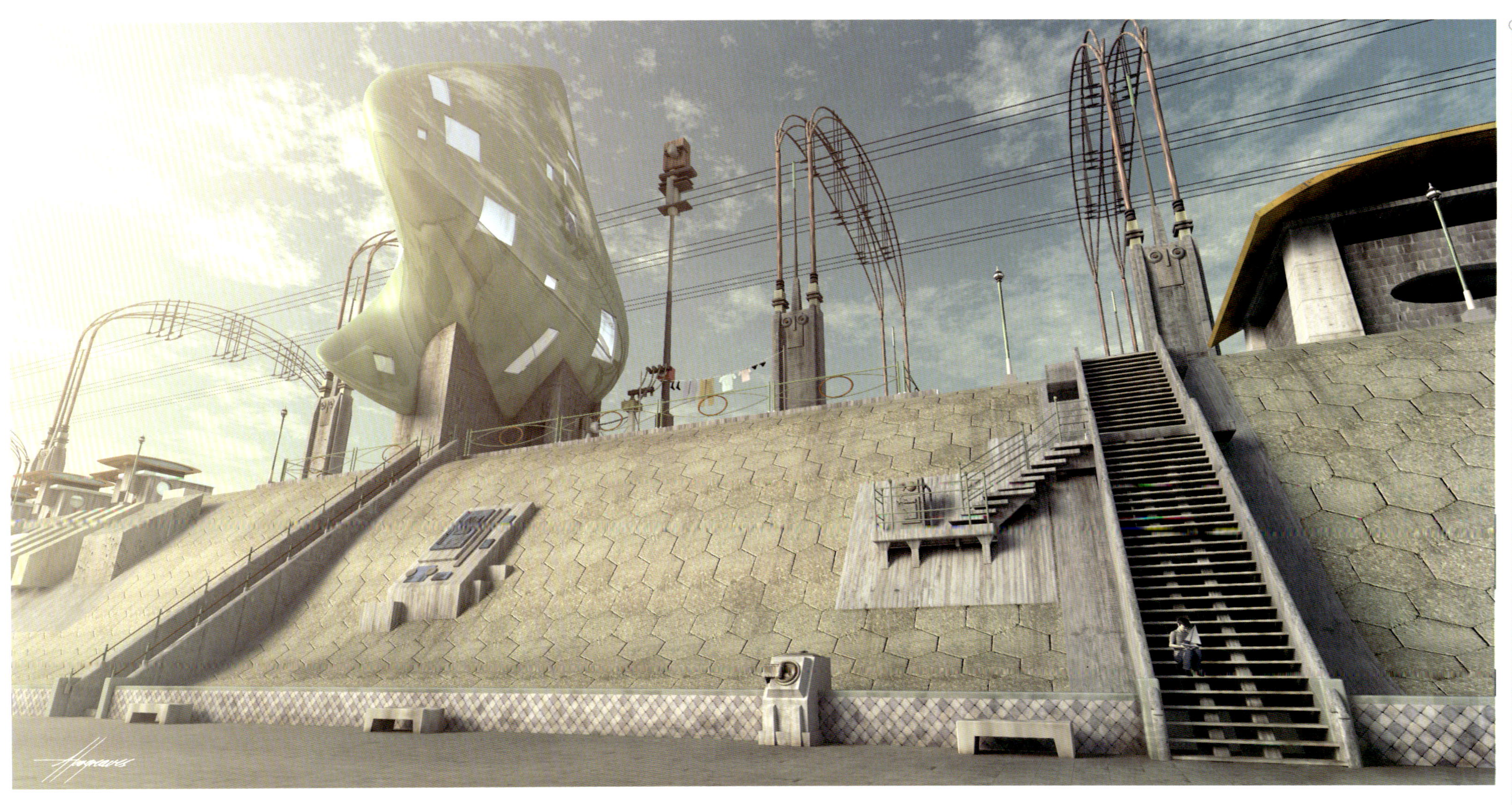

RAILROAD HOUSE
4500 x 2250 pixels

22

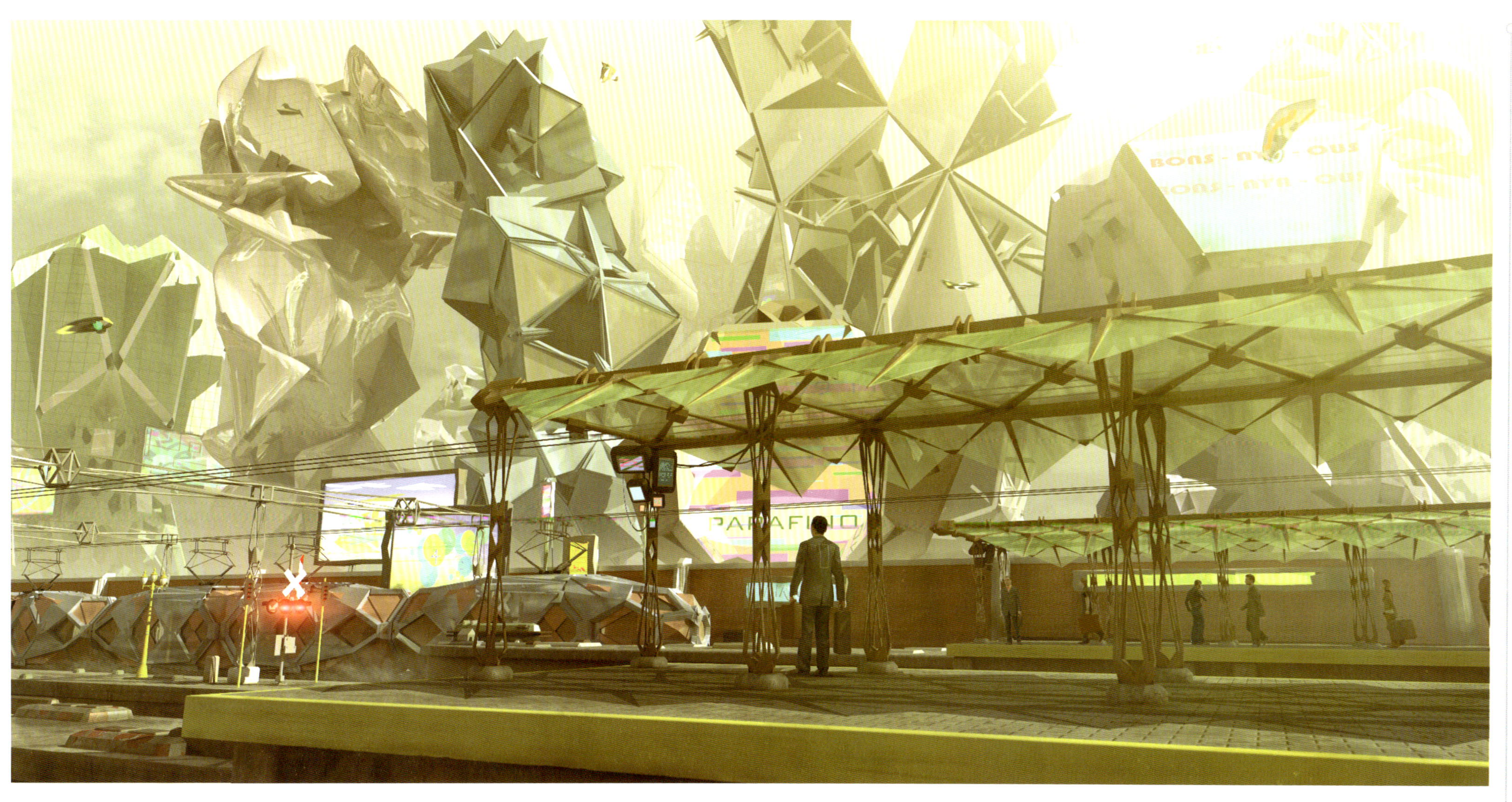

EASTERN EXPRESS FROM THE PLAINS OF LAPRIDUS ON THE
MORNING OF THE SEVENTH TIDE OF HENREKI POSJ

2500 x 1250 pixels

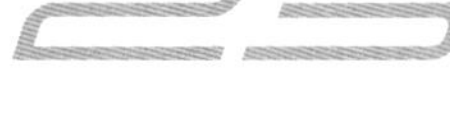

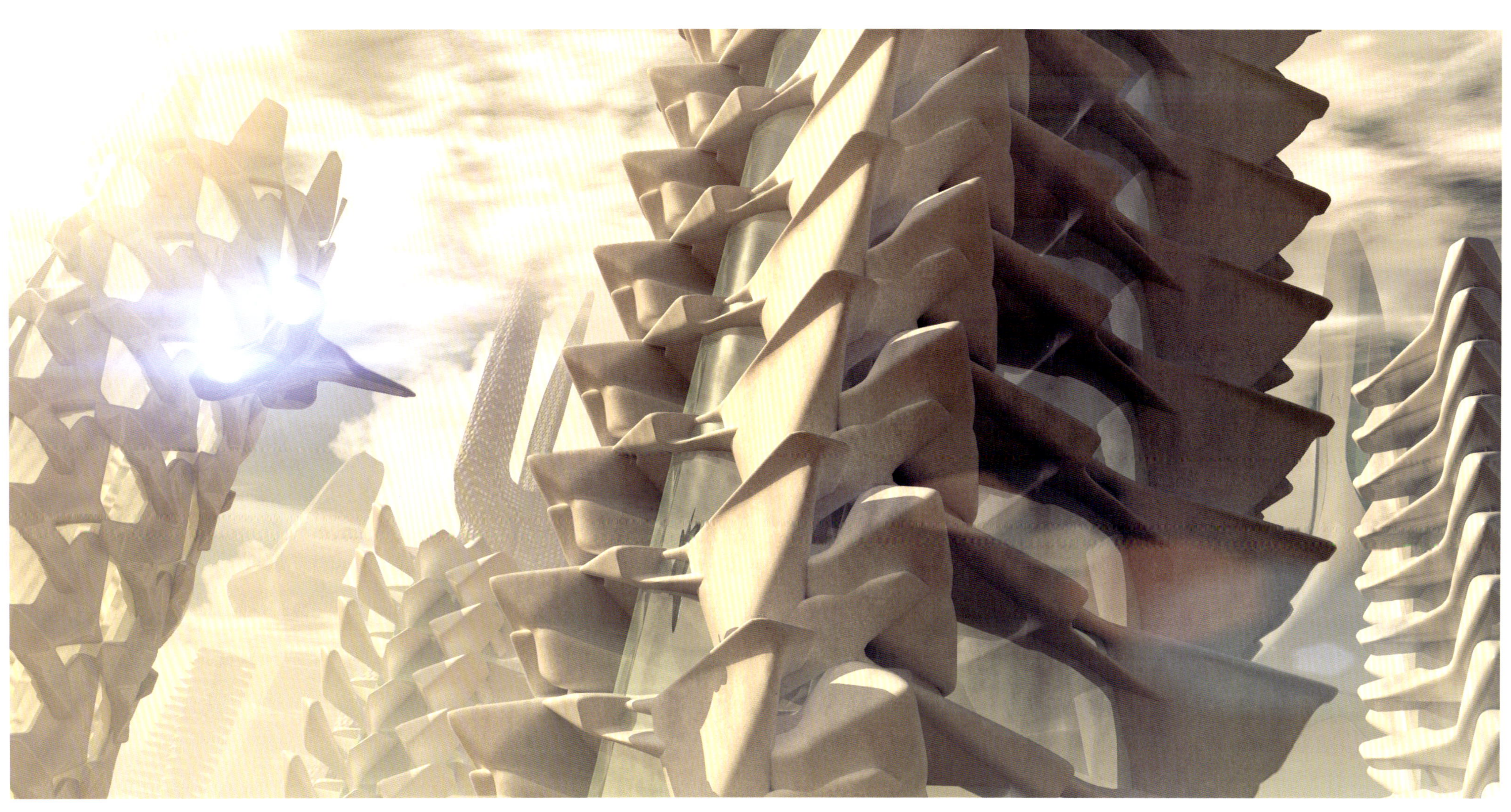

BONE
3000 x 1500 pixels

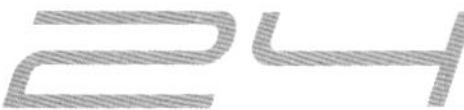

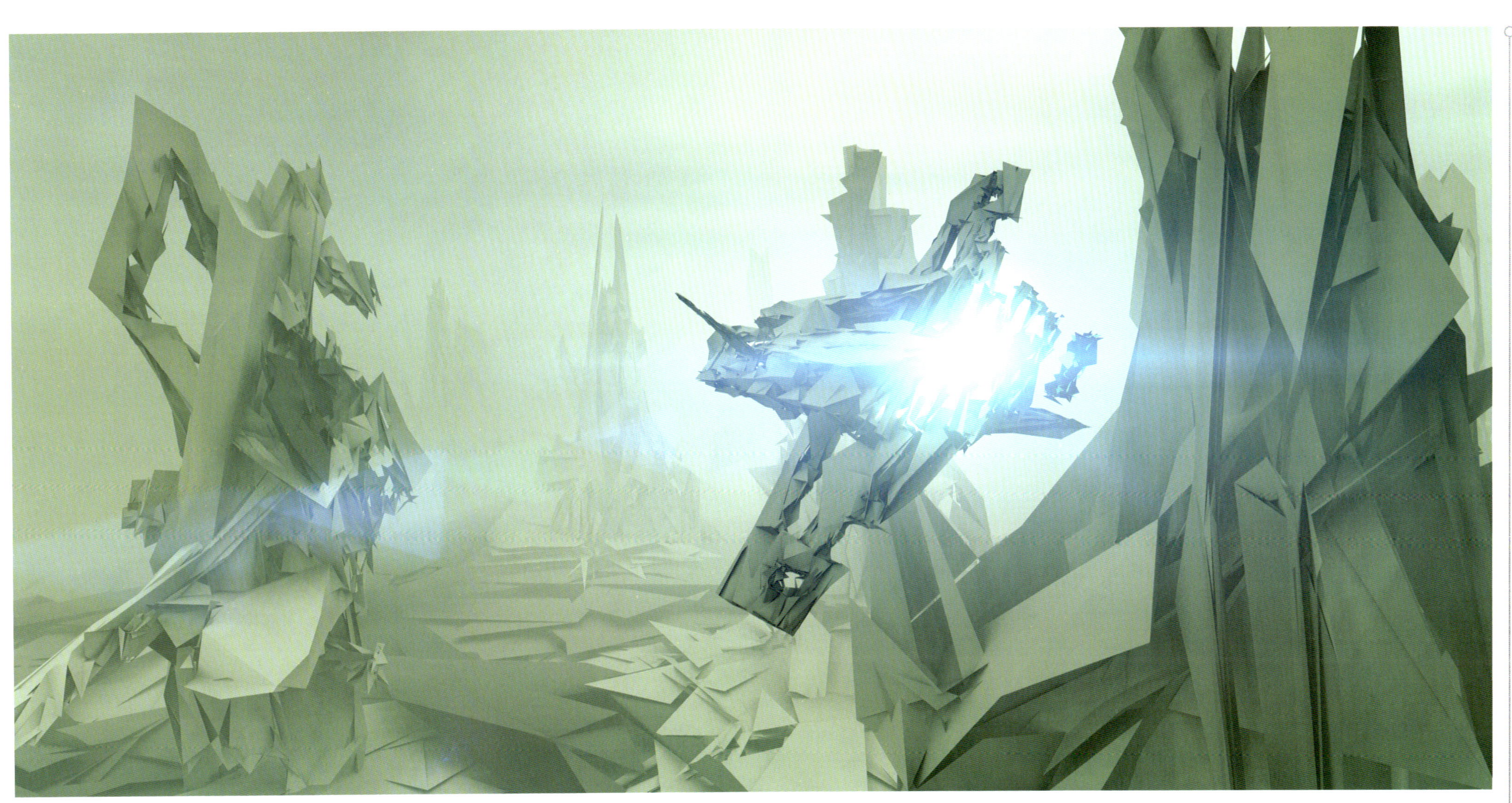

SHARD
4000 x 2000 pixels

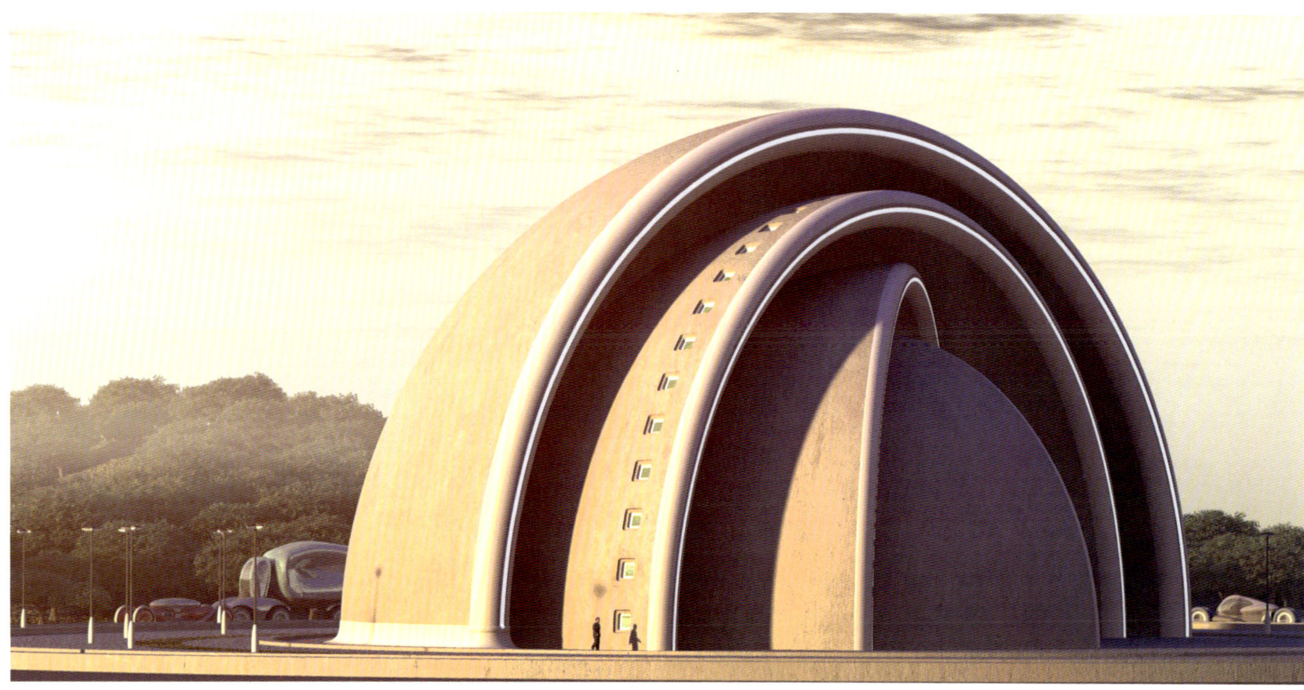

25

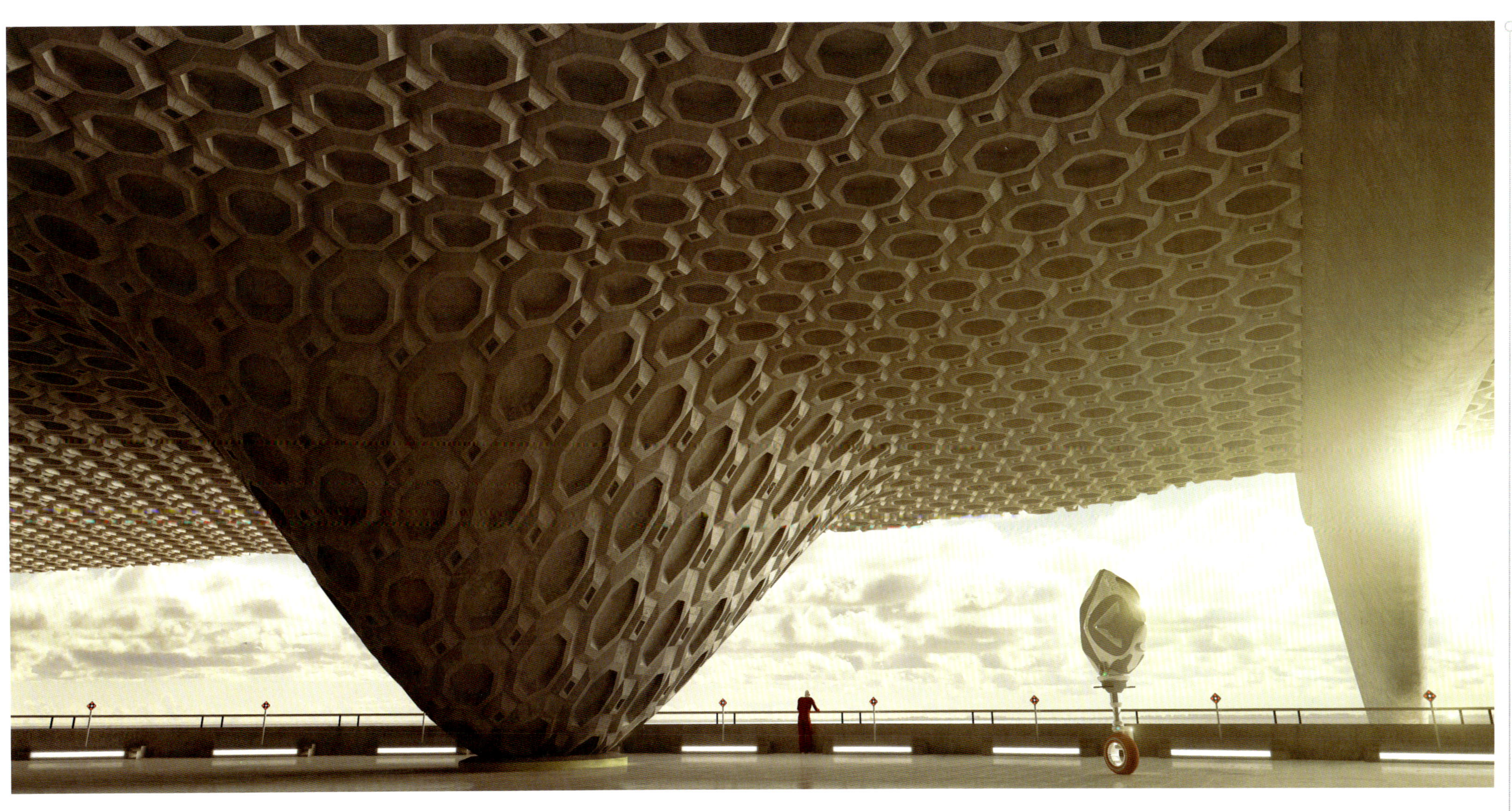

26

LIGHT TO LIGHT
3000 x 1500 pixels

27

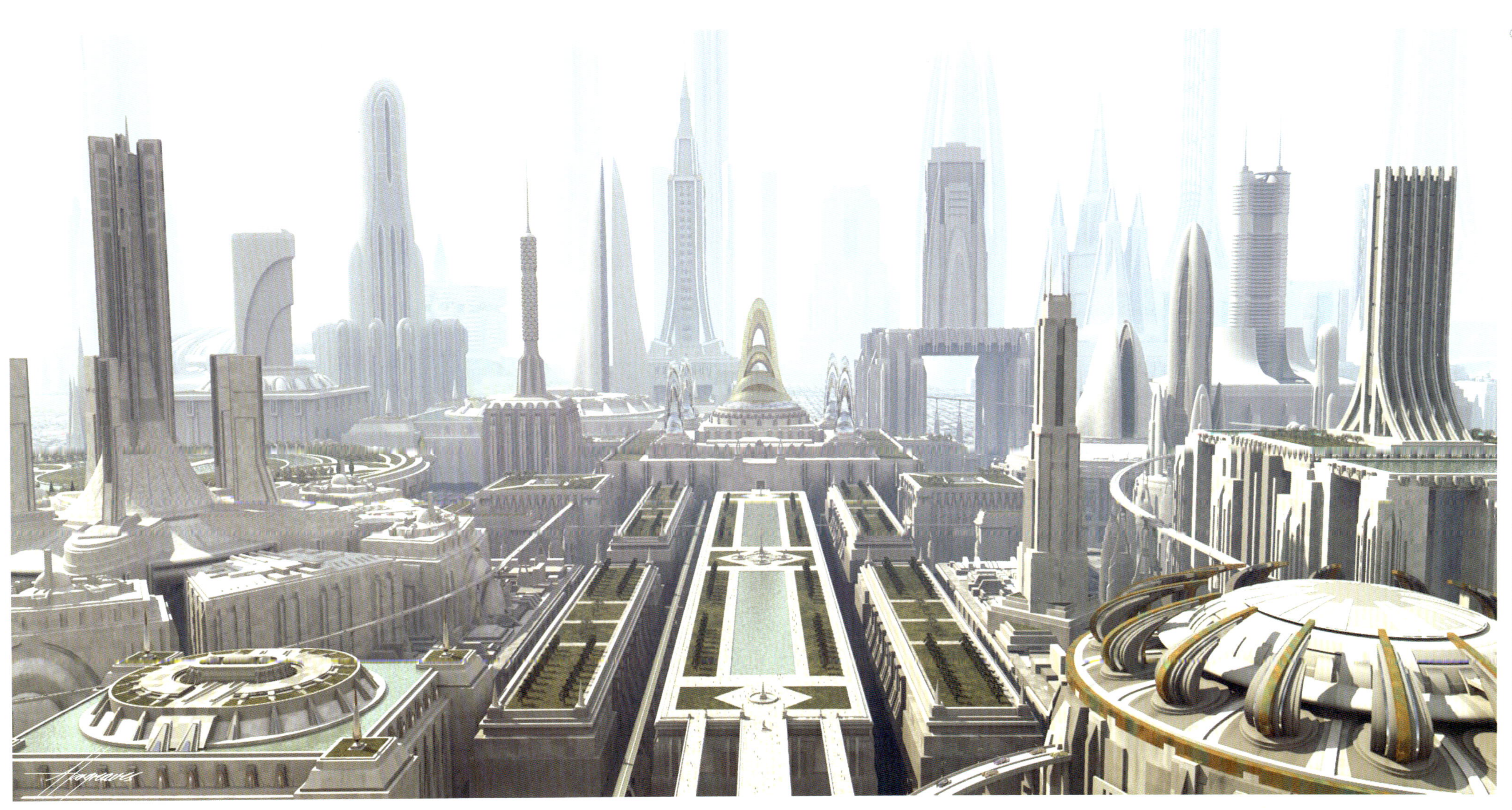

SEHLEROM
3000 x 1500 pixels
SEÁN HARGREAVES : PLACES

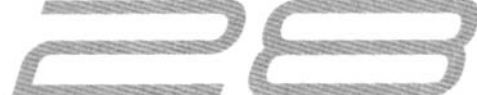

With repetition comes strength. The interlocked latticework idea was common in the 1950's and 1960's, and in this image I took the complexity to another level. Here in Los Angeles the light is very hard and sharp, and there are many buildings whose detail and surfaces are defined by this light. I'm in favor of continuing this type of detailing in architecture as, like Art Deco, I feel it wasn't taken far enough in its concept, and with the advent of engineering software we are aided in being able to push building concepts to a much higher level than ever before.

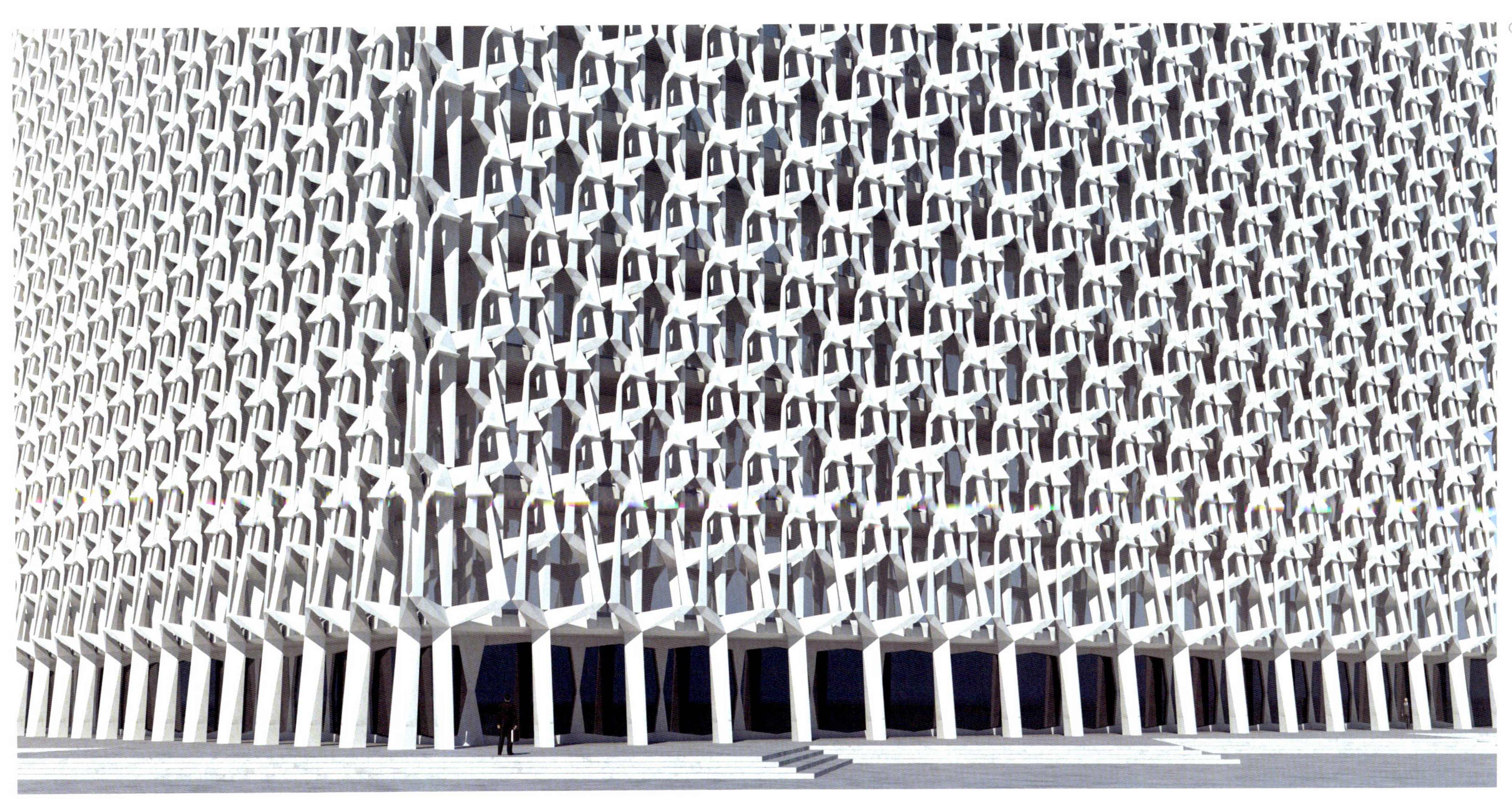

CORNER OF A BUILDING

3000 x 1500 pixels

29

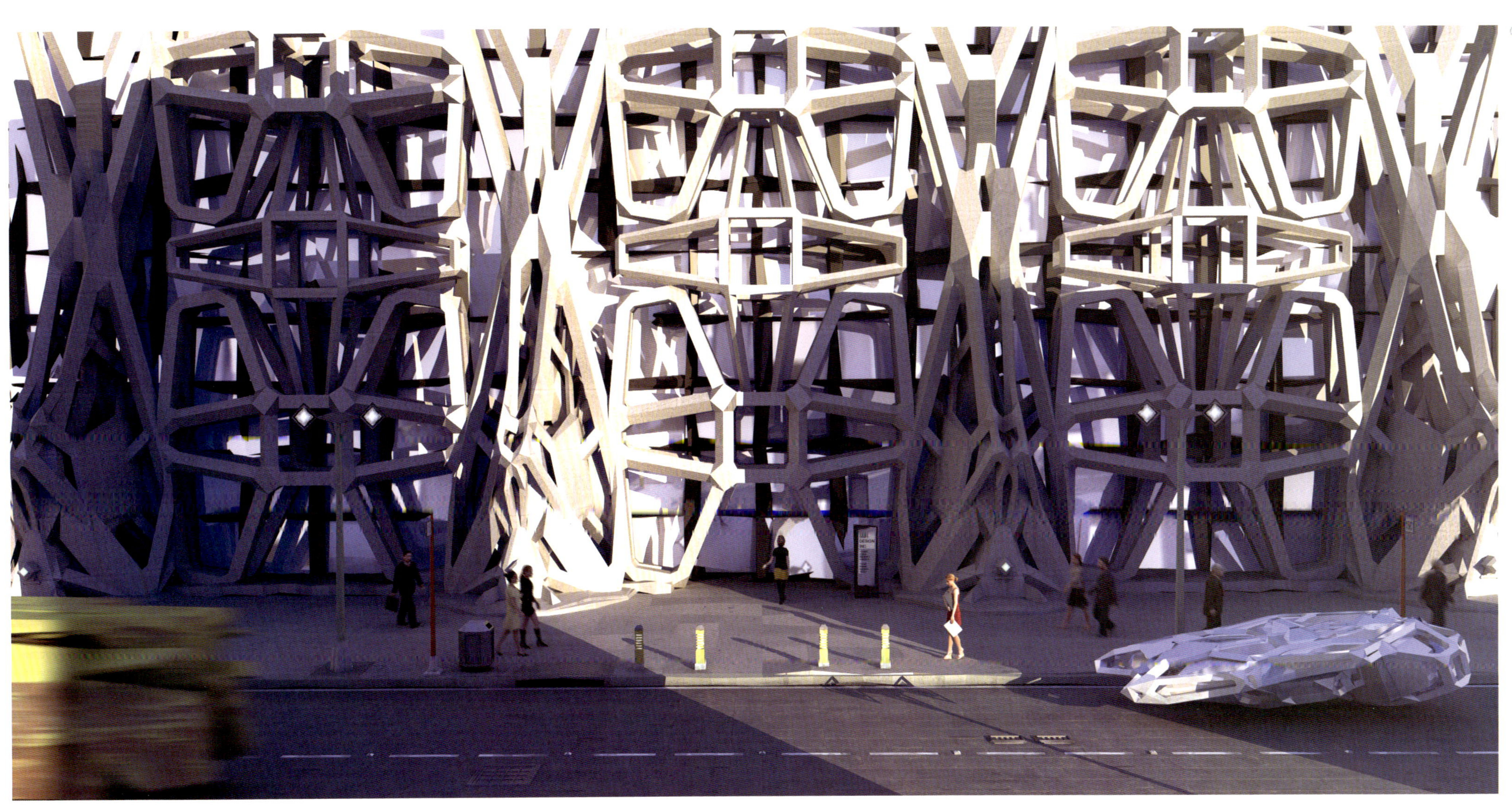
REVRECLEHAN
3000 x 1500 pixels

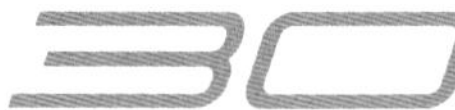

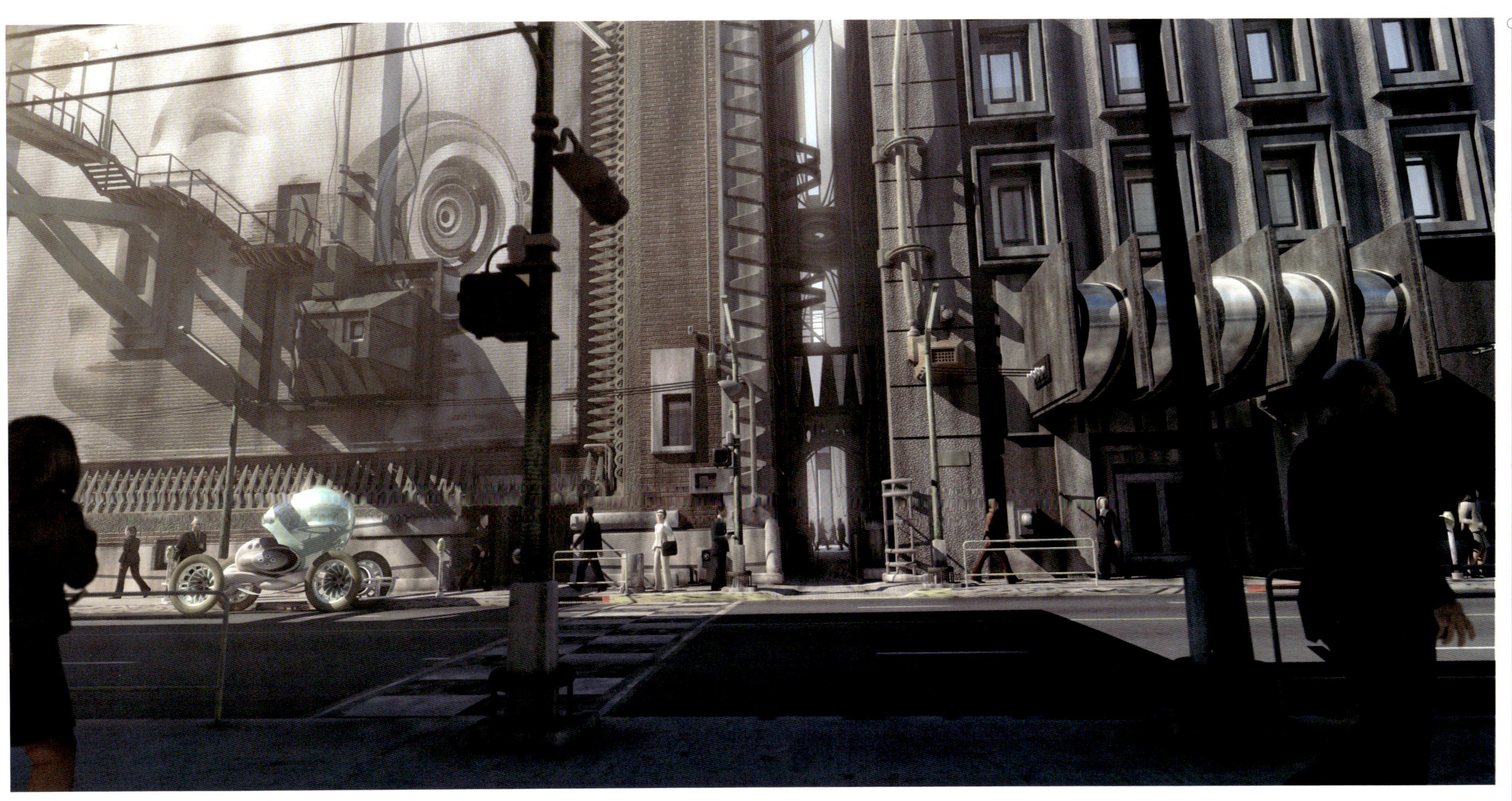

KNOWN AND UNKNOWN
4000 x 2000 pixels

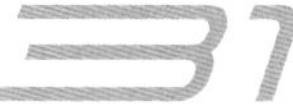

There aren't many straight lines or flat surfaces in this image. I wanted to break every flat surface into a kind of facet, or offset plane. Streets are interesting subjects, as there are many details we take for granted such as access panels, or replaced surfaces. A street grows from its initial build over time, where things are added and taken away, painted, and then painted over.

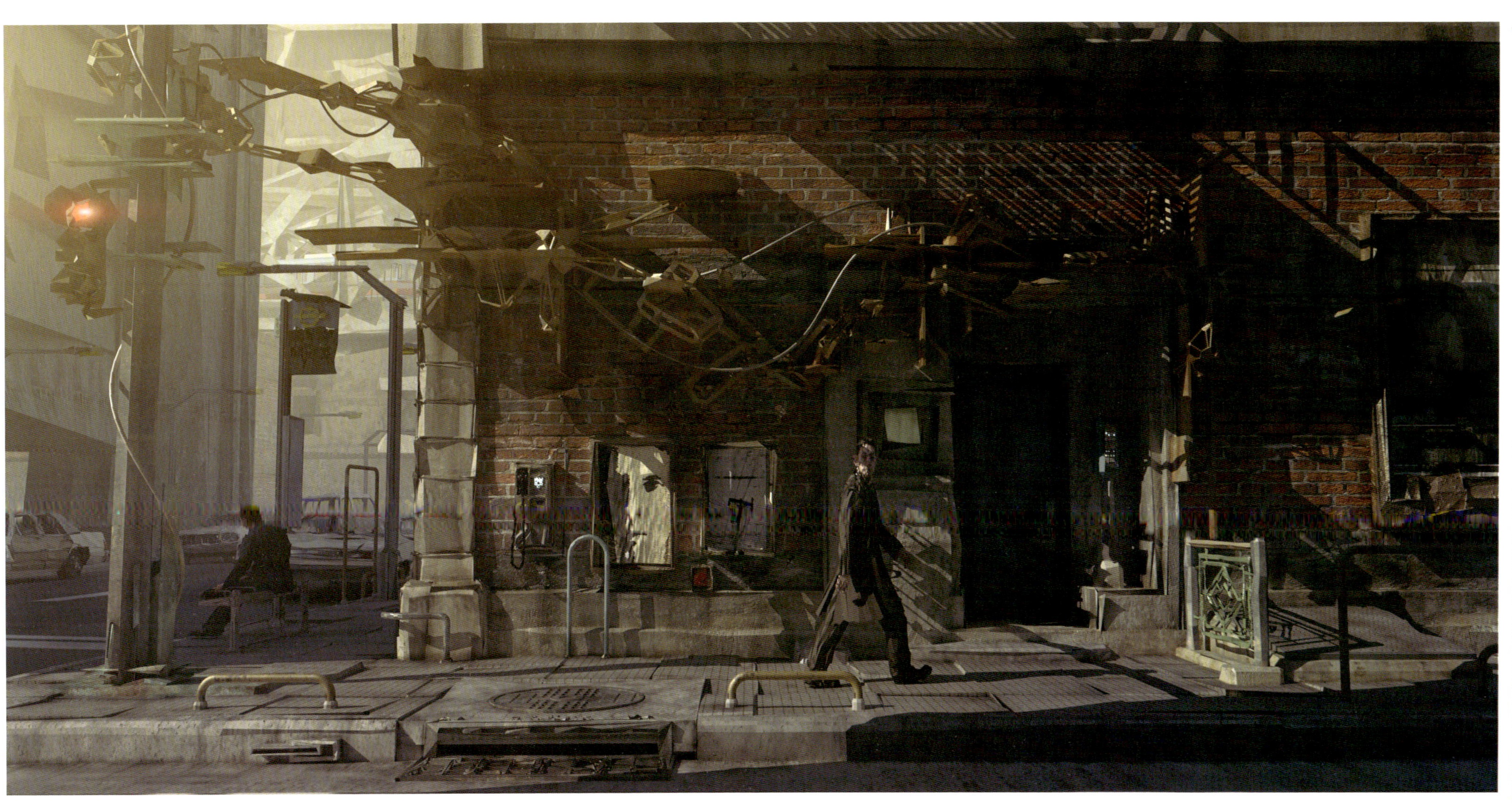

CORNER DOOR

3000 x 1500 pixels

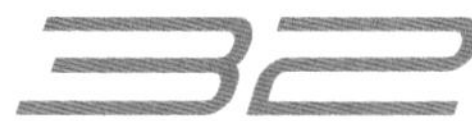

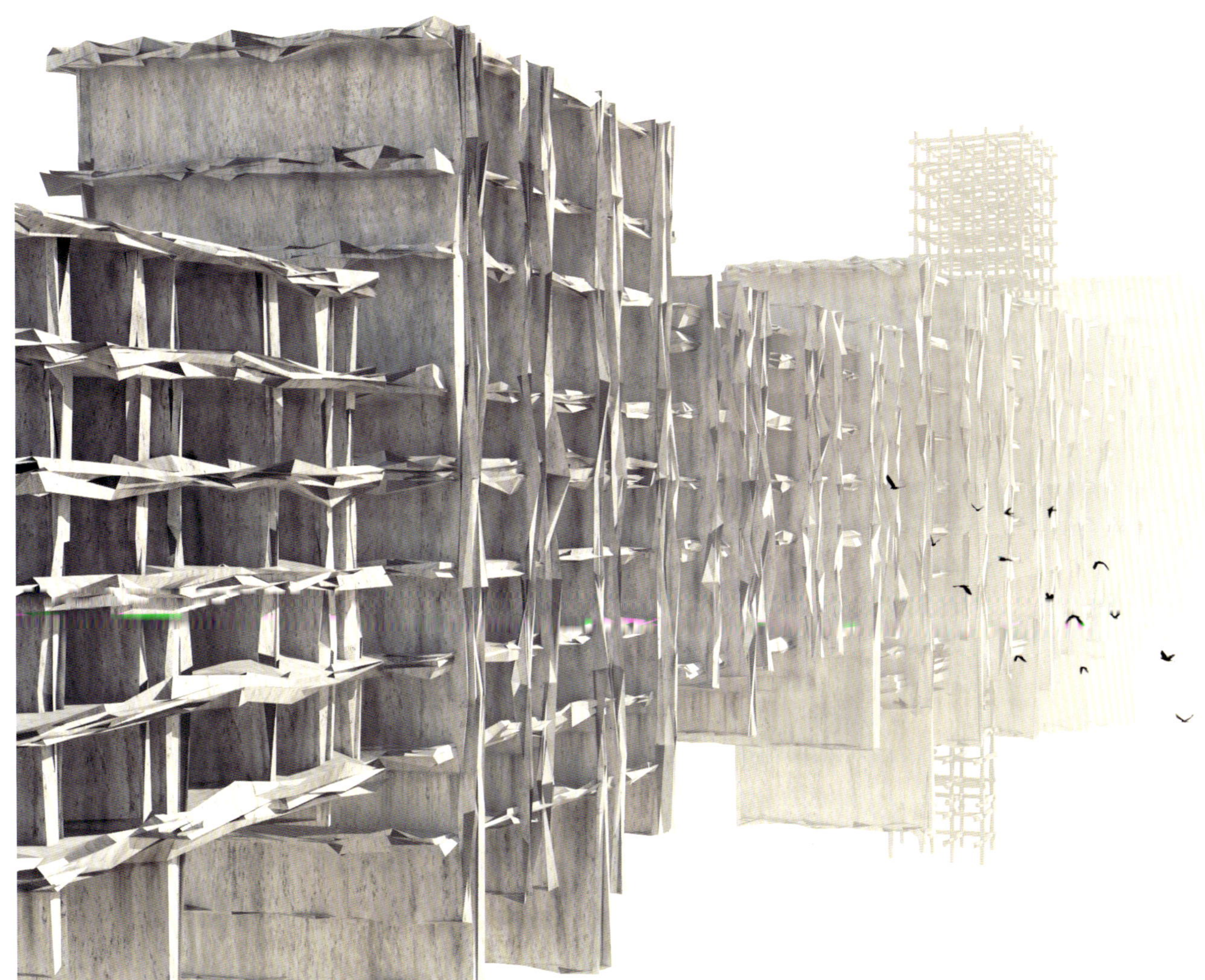
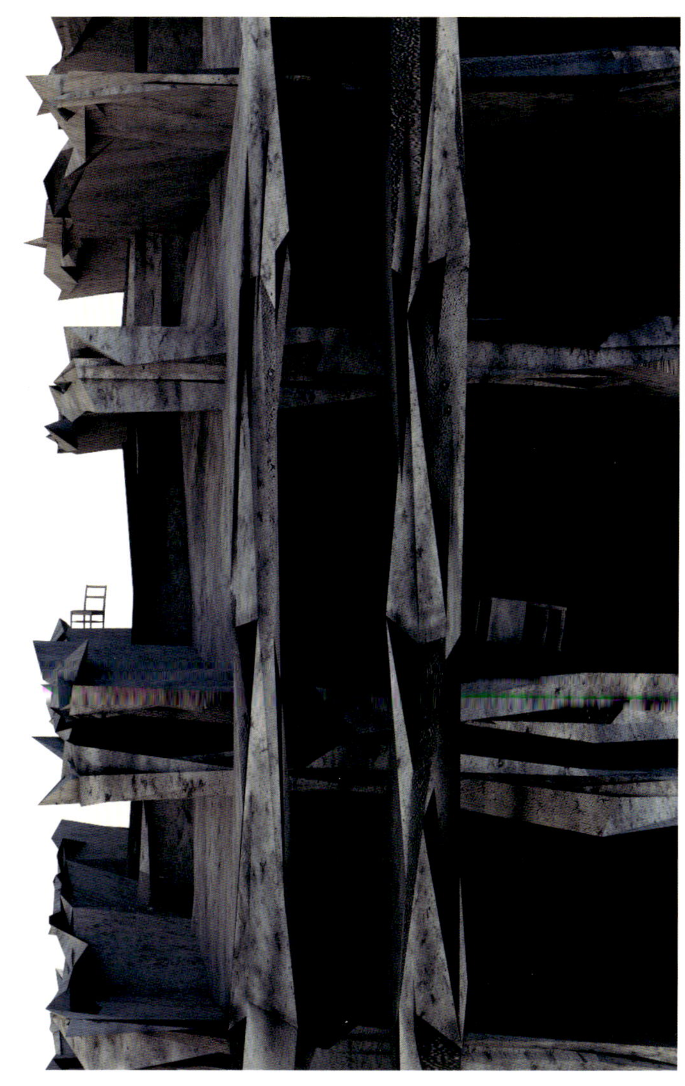

FLOATING RUINS
3000 x 1500 pixels

33

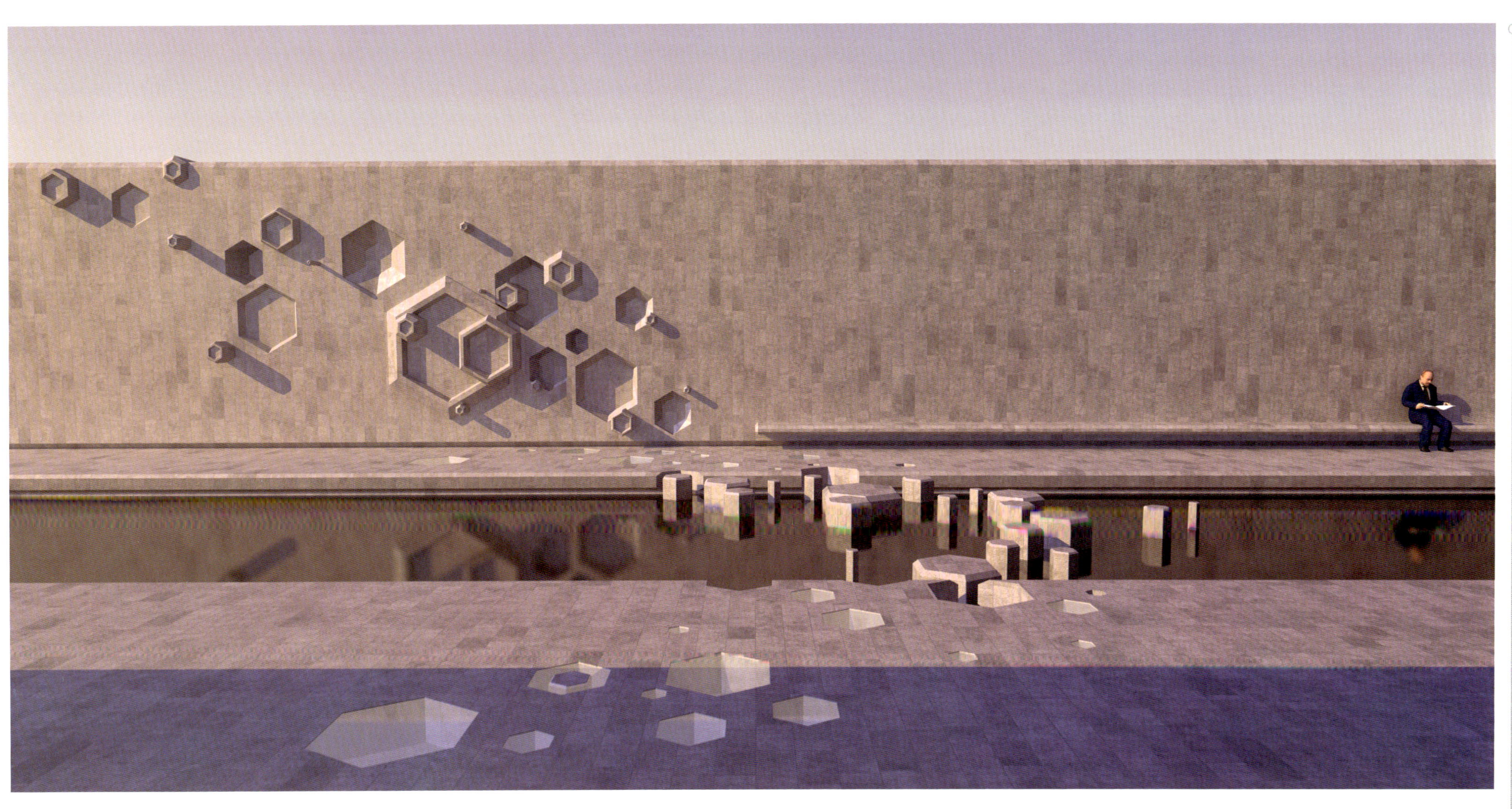

HECTAGON GARDEN
3000 x 1500 pixels

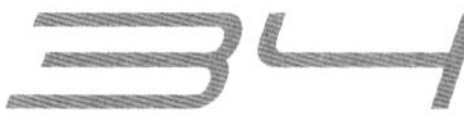

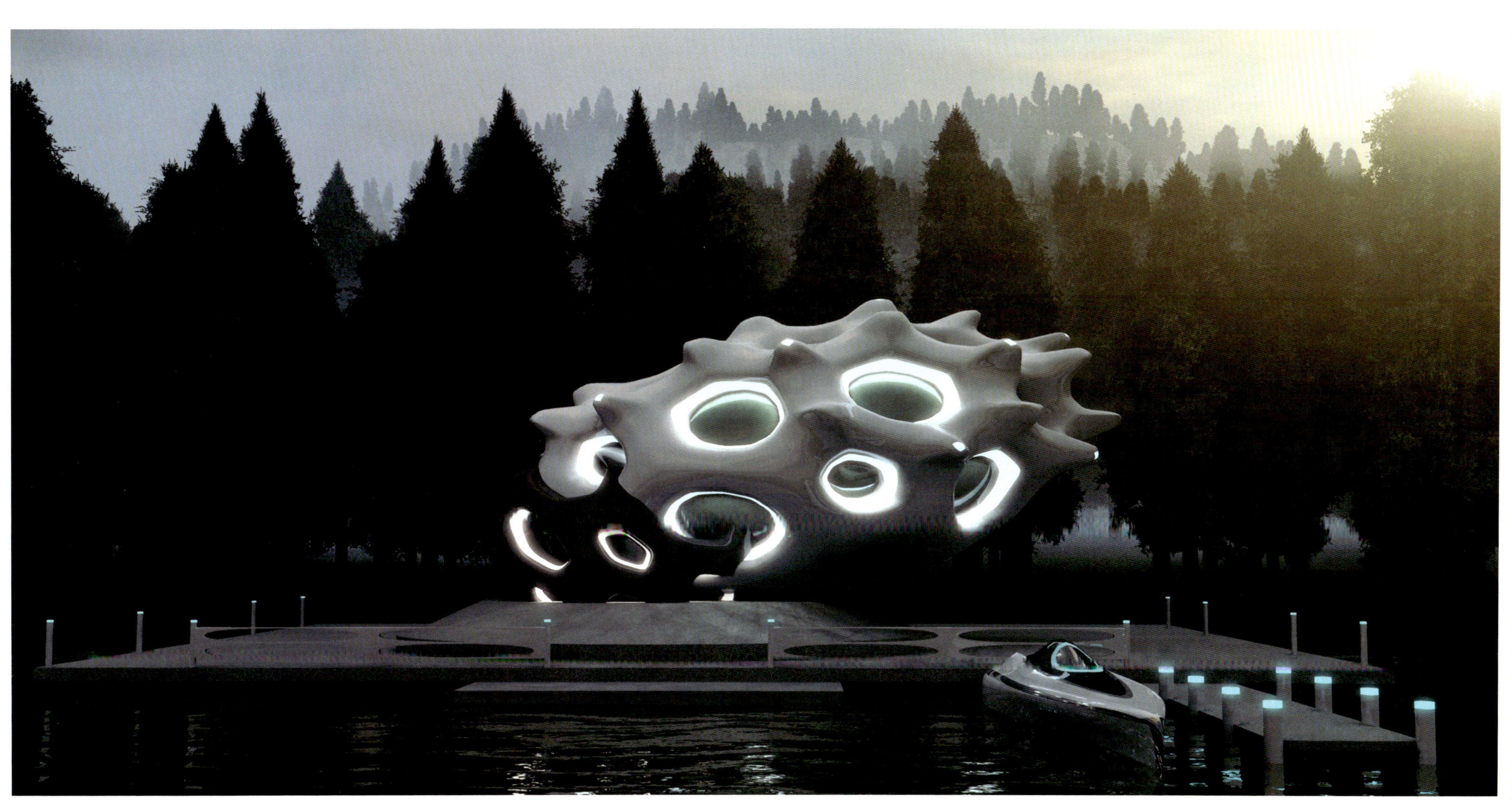

FOREST HOUSE
3000 x 1500 pixels
SEÁN HARGREAVES : PLACES

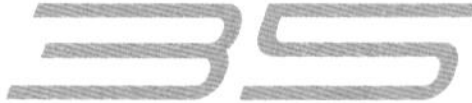

The room is a puzzle, a space the man can escape from if he discovers the way. He is sitting at the table holding the Hexadecorelimus, a kind of faceted sphere. Each surface in the room can aid him in his escape, but only the object in his hand unlocks the way.

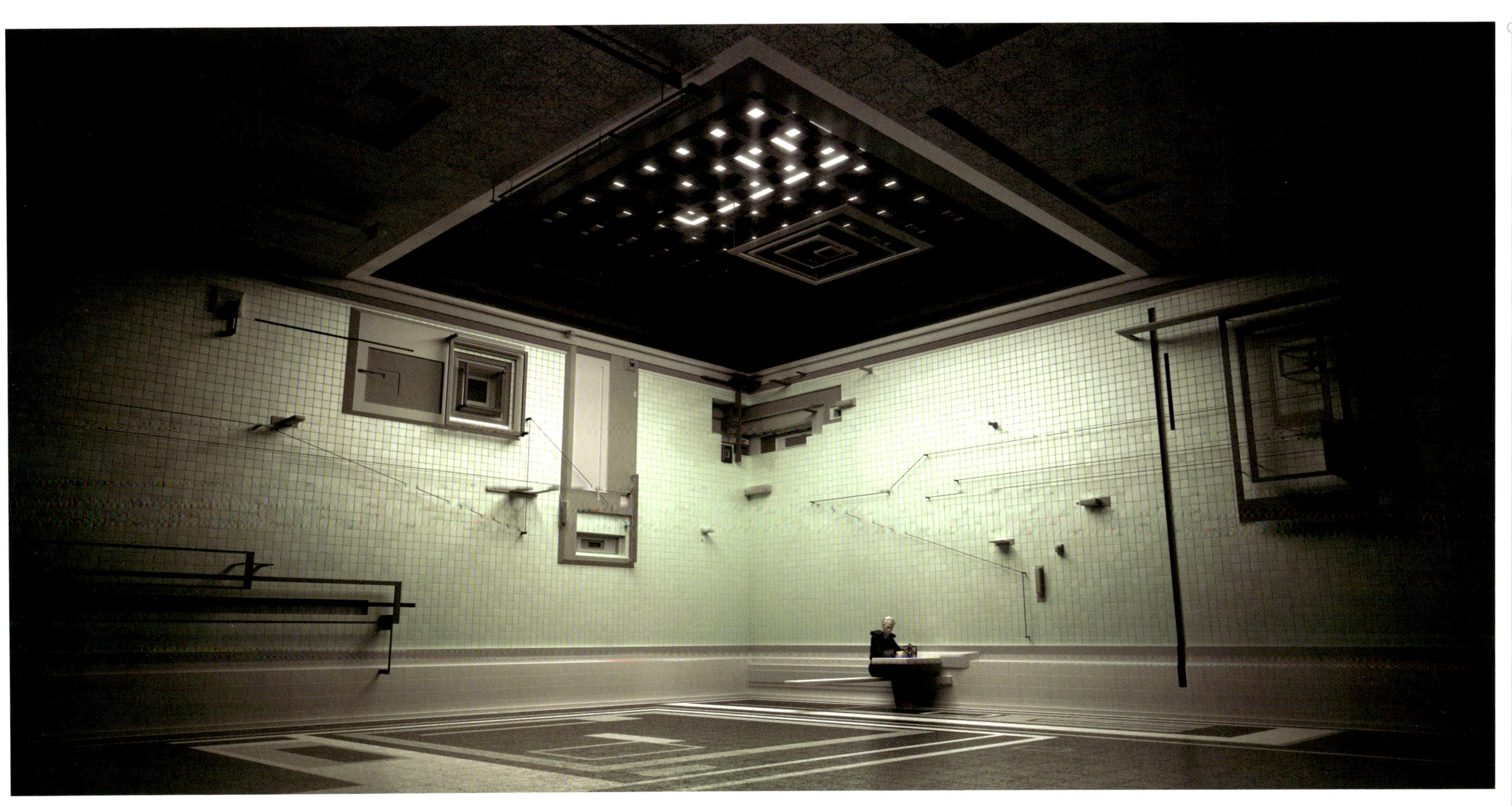

QUANTELLES

3000 x 1500 pixels

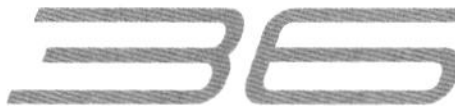

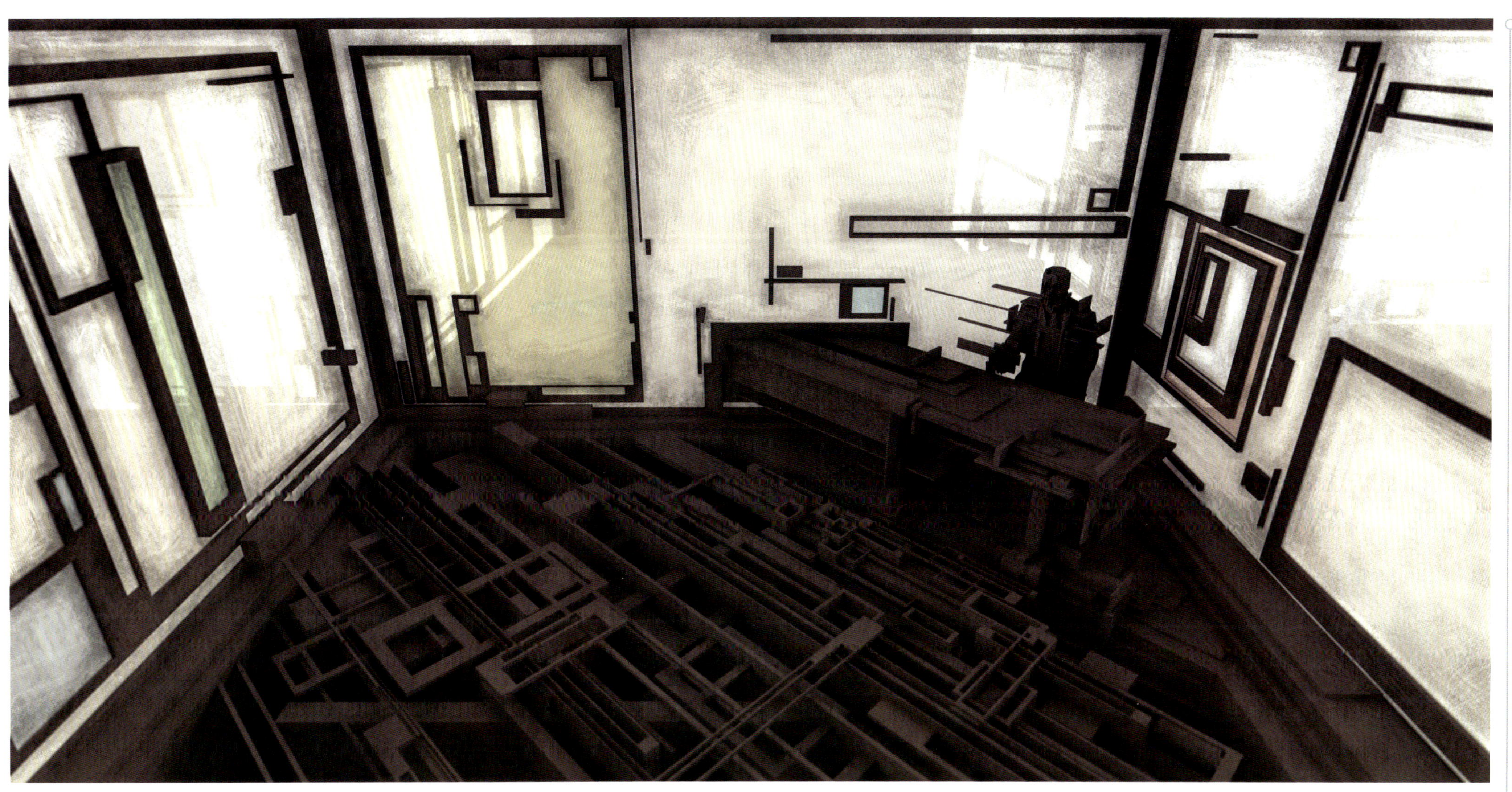

HERMETICAL

3000 x 1500 pixels

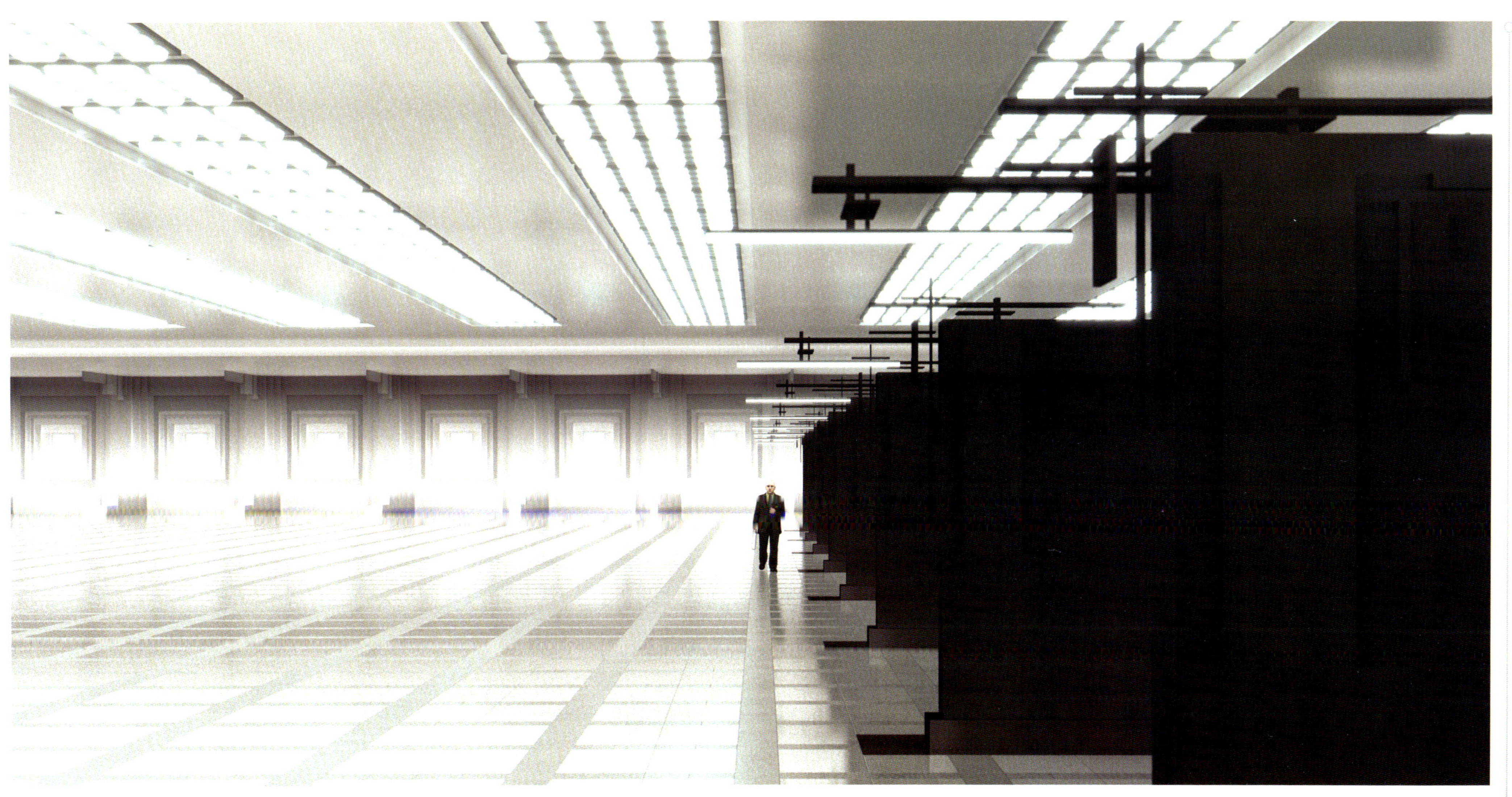

NEVAELS.
3000 x 1500 pixels

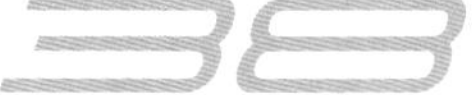

To me, an empty, modern, minimalist room is a welcome place. Away from the visual and audio clutter we see and hear every day. In this image I like the juxtaposition of the lack of surface detail below the top of the wall, as opposed to what is above that plane. There's always a balance in architecture in terms of 'visual weight' that is hard to define as well as achieve.

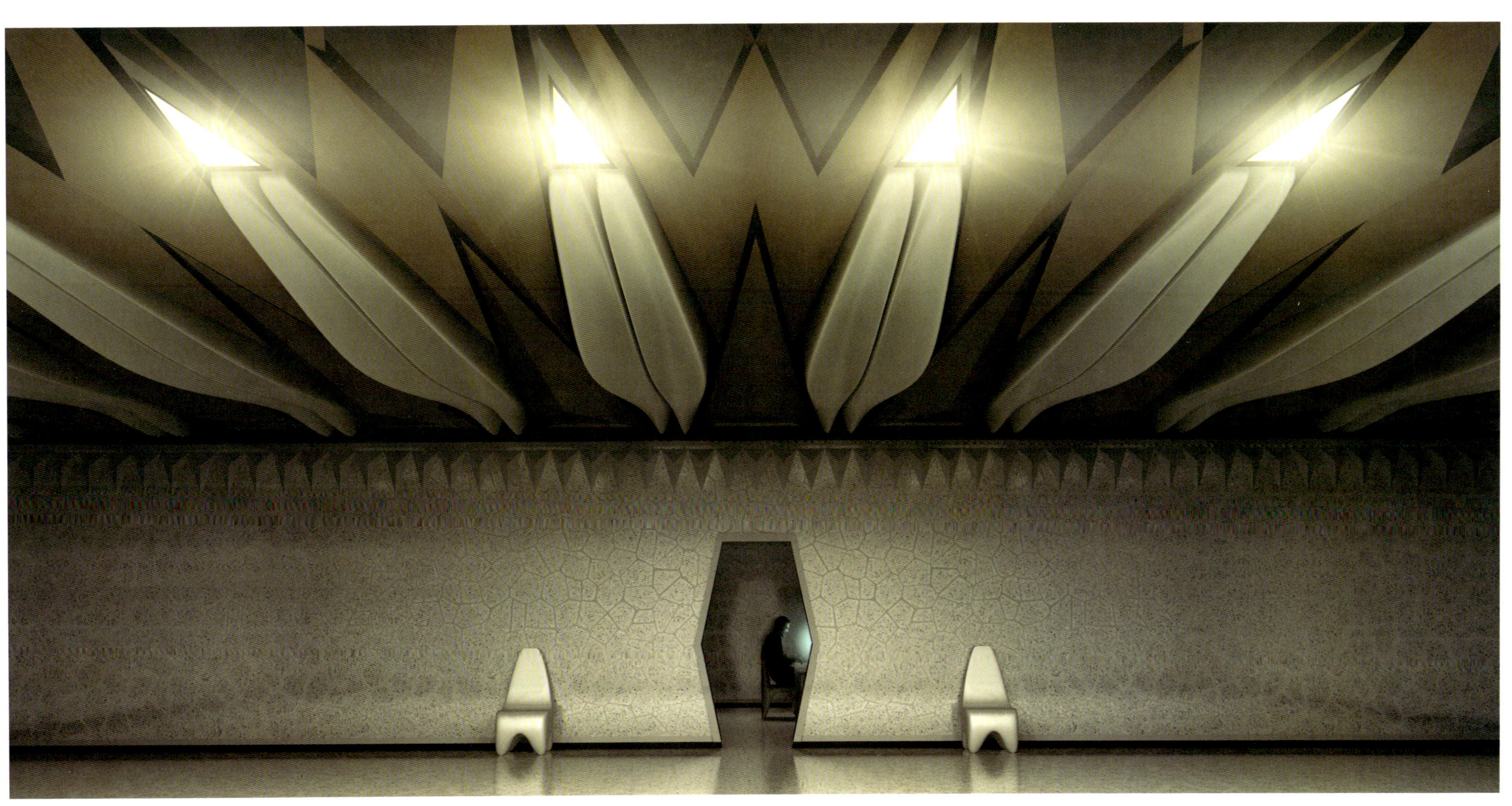

ROOM

3000 x 1500 pixels

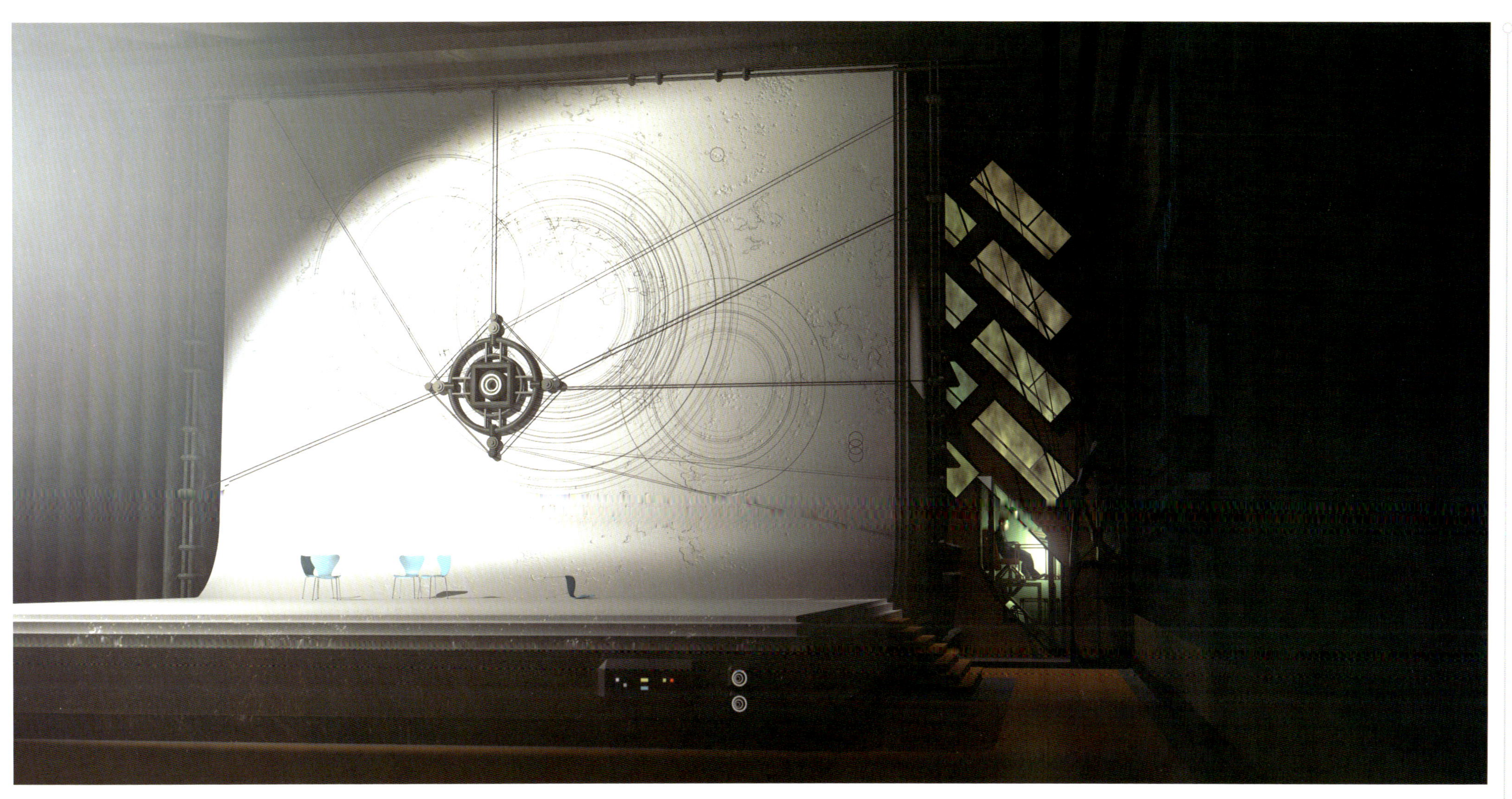

AFTER THE SHOW

3000 x 1500 pixels

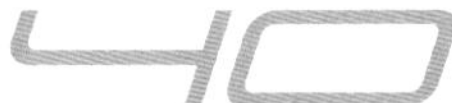

I've spent many hours in museums and galleries, and I'm interested in many types of art, including non-representational works. Here is a room of a few pieces, but is it a gallery, or some place in the future? To me it doesn't matter. What does matter is that it seems like a peaceful, interesting place. It makes you think, and the parts of the whole make you stare a little.

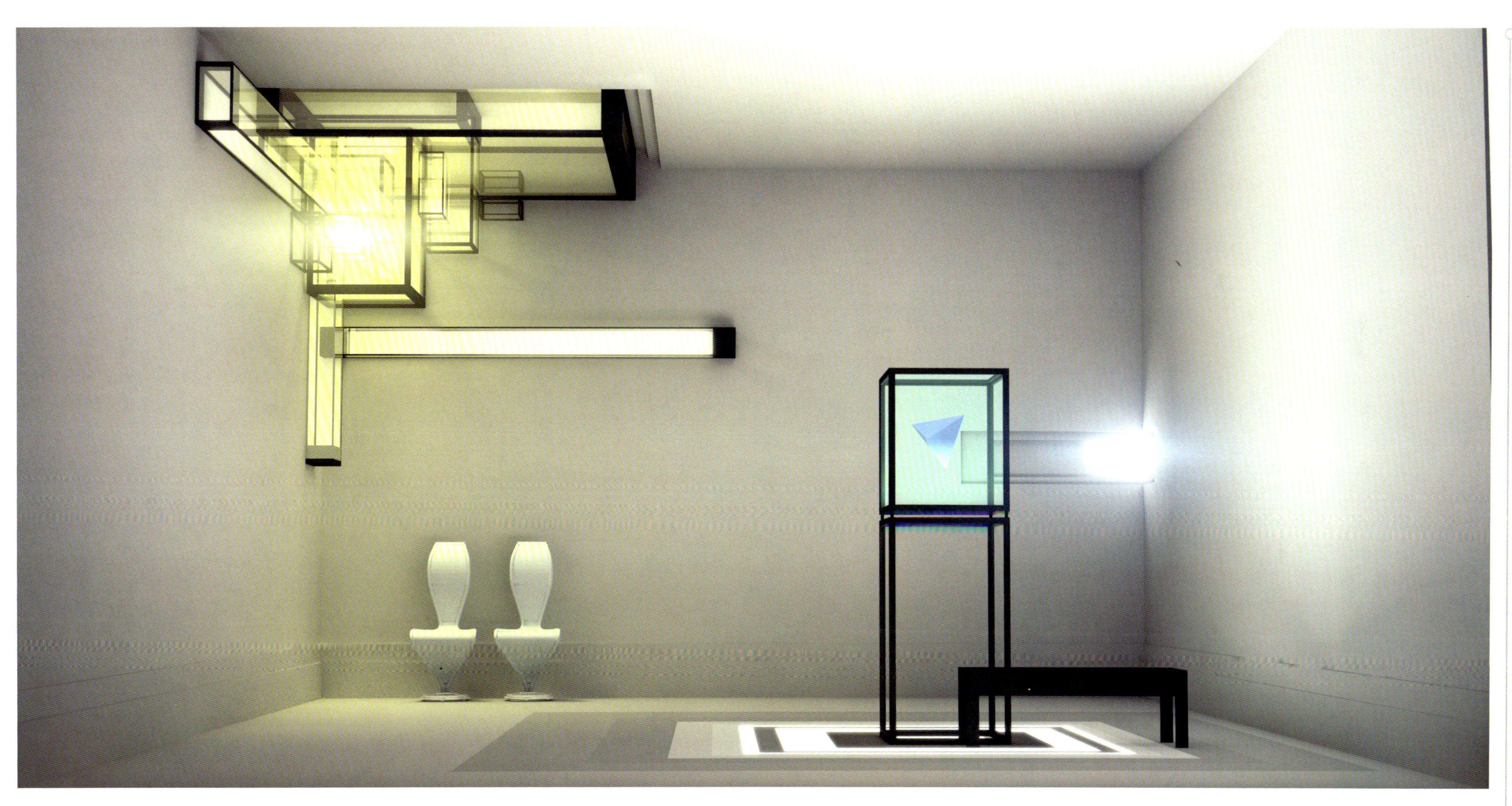
BLOCK GLASS
4000 x 2000 pixels
SEÁN HARGREAVES : PLACES

47

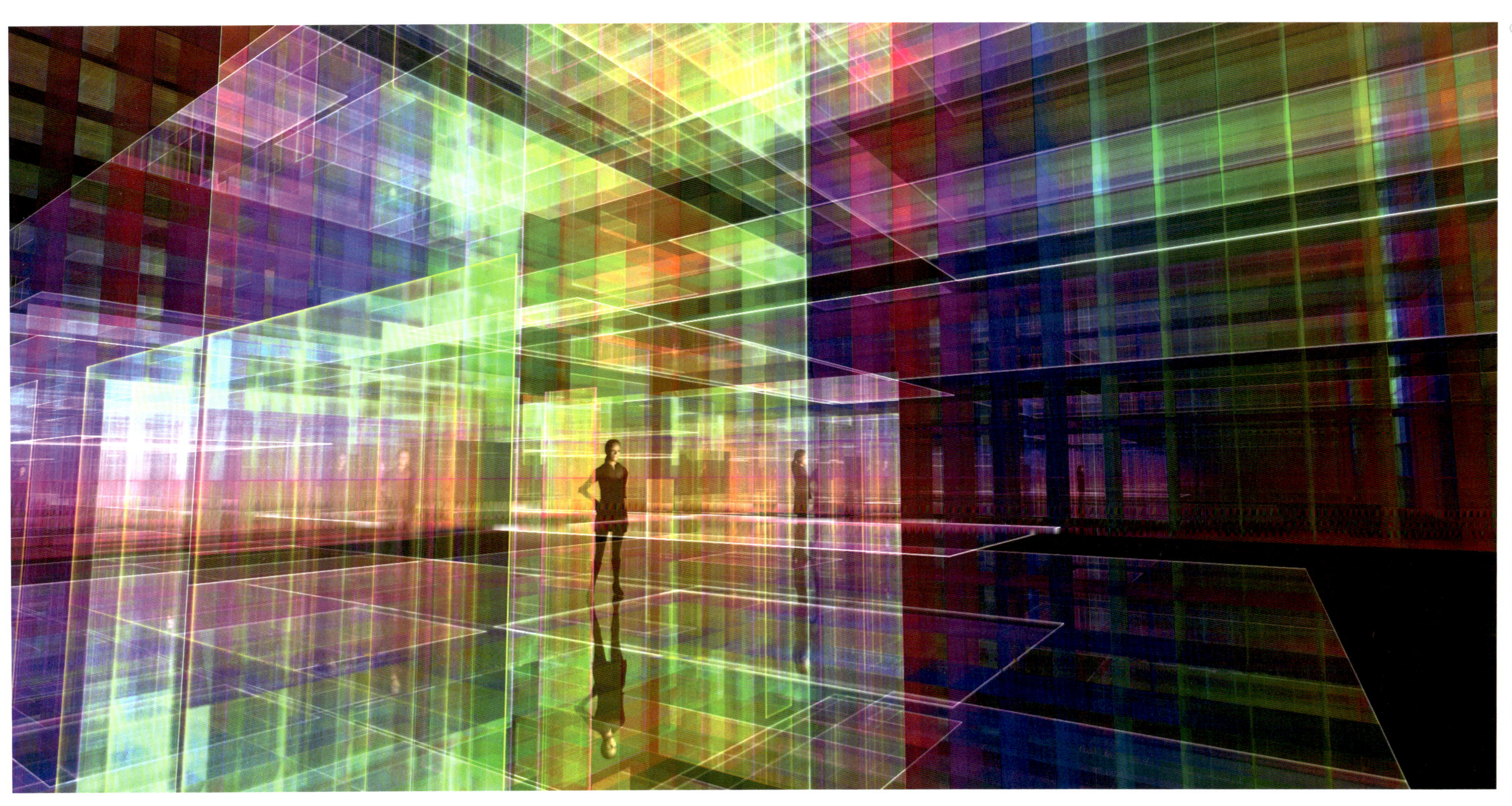
A-REPLEMENTALIC-A
2500 x 1250 pixels

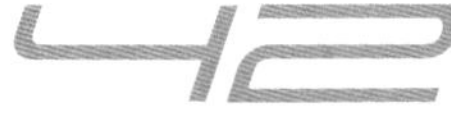

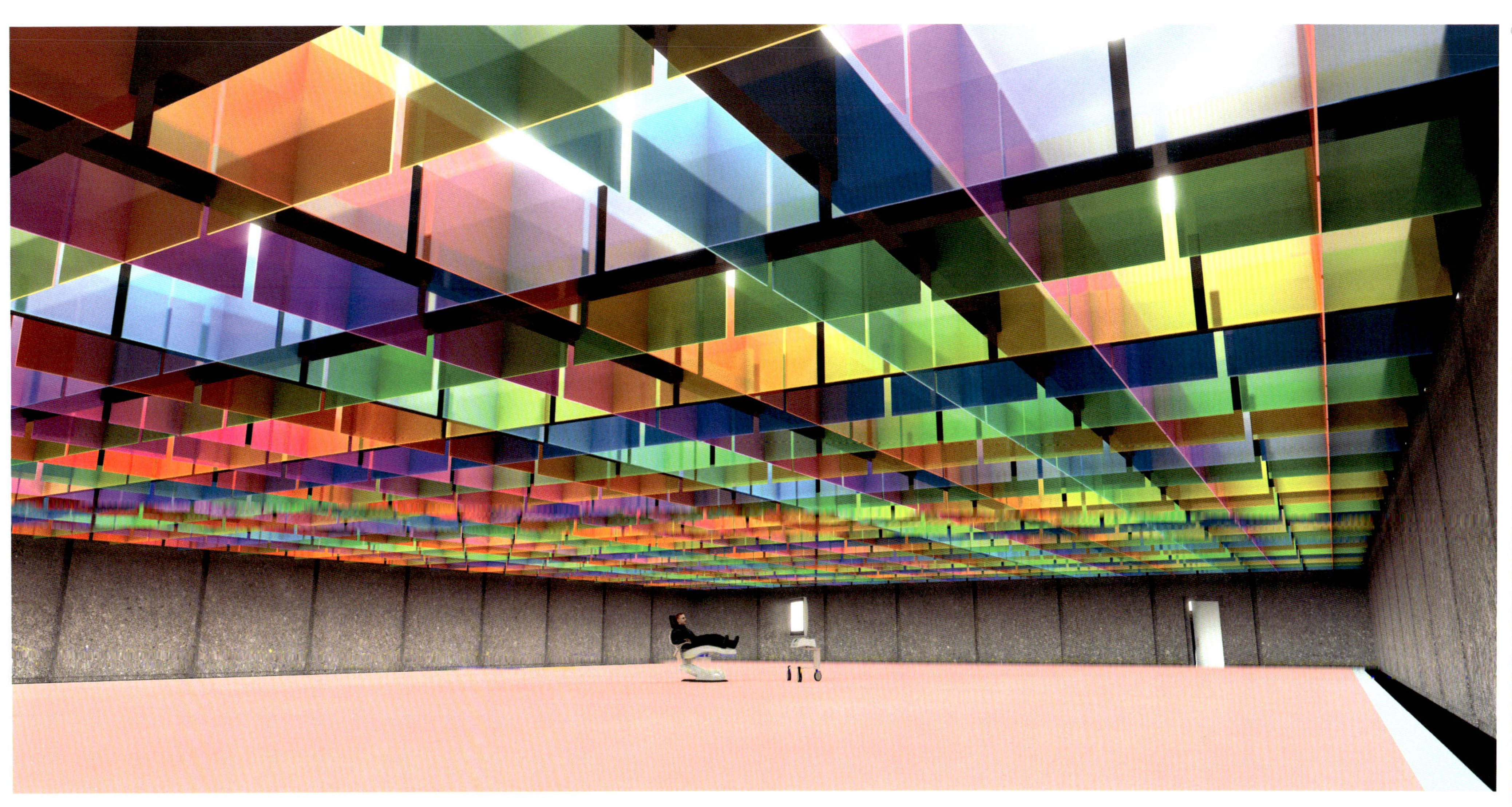

CHANNEL O
3000 x 1500 pixels
SEÁN HARGREAVES : PLACES

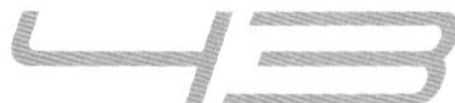

When I was young I had a building set of colored plastic sheets that fit together, and I made all kinds of things with them. I was fascinated by the light passing through the colors and how the colors changed relative to the light. Here I've shown a corridor with that same feeling, while at the same time the long lens and compressed depth of field gives it an almost abstract painting effect.

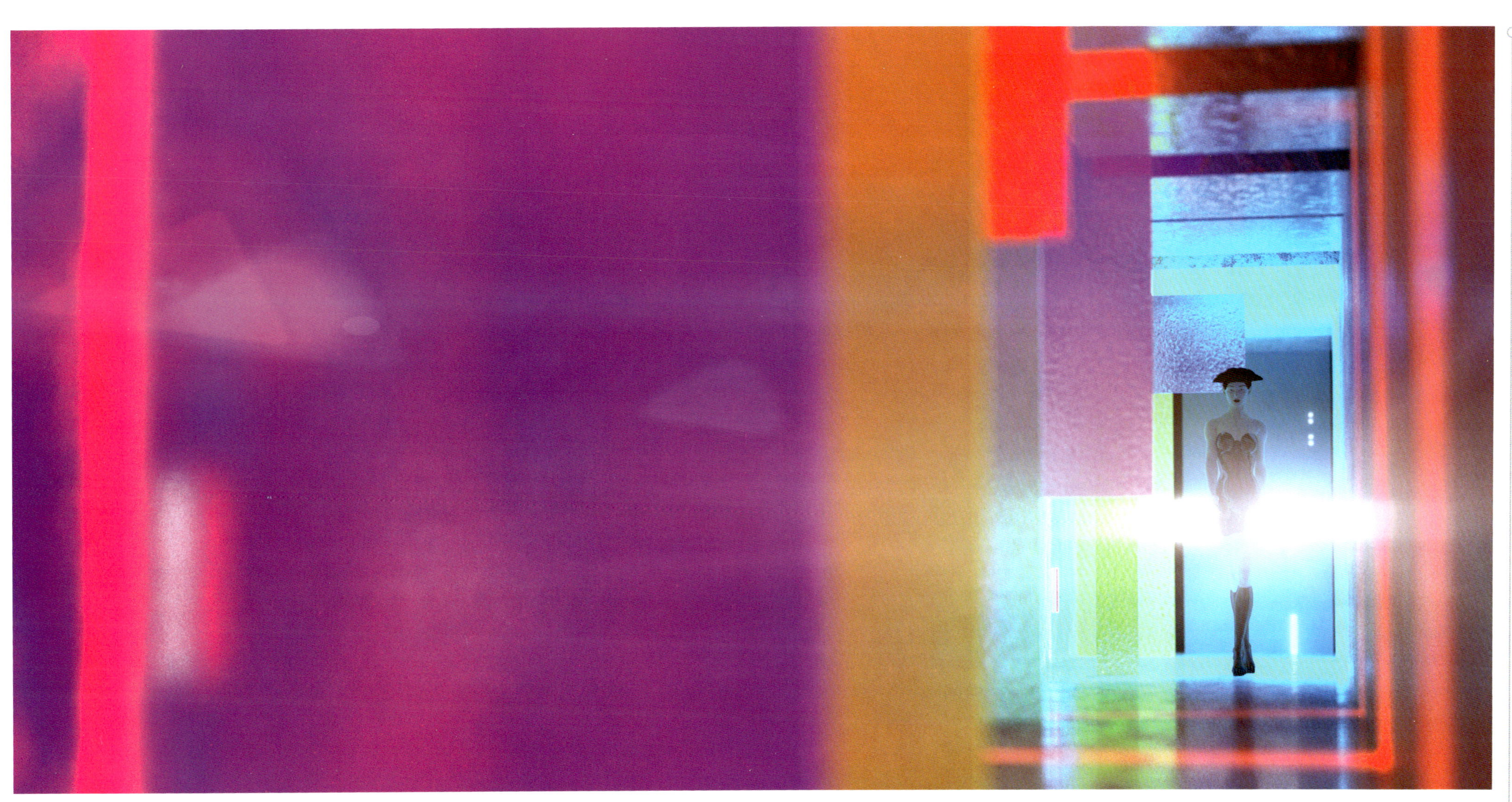

HI - FLAVRELICUS

3000 x 1500 pixels

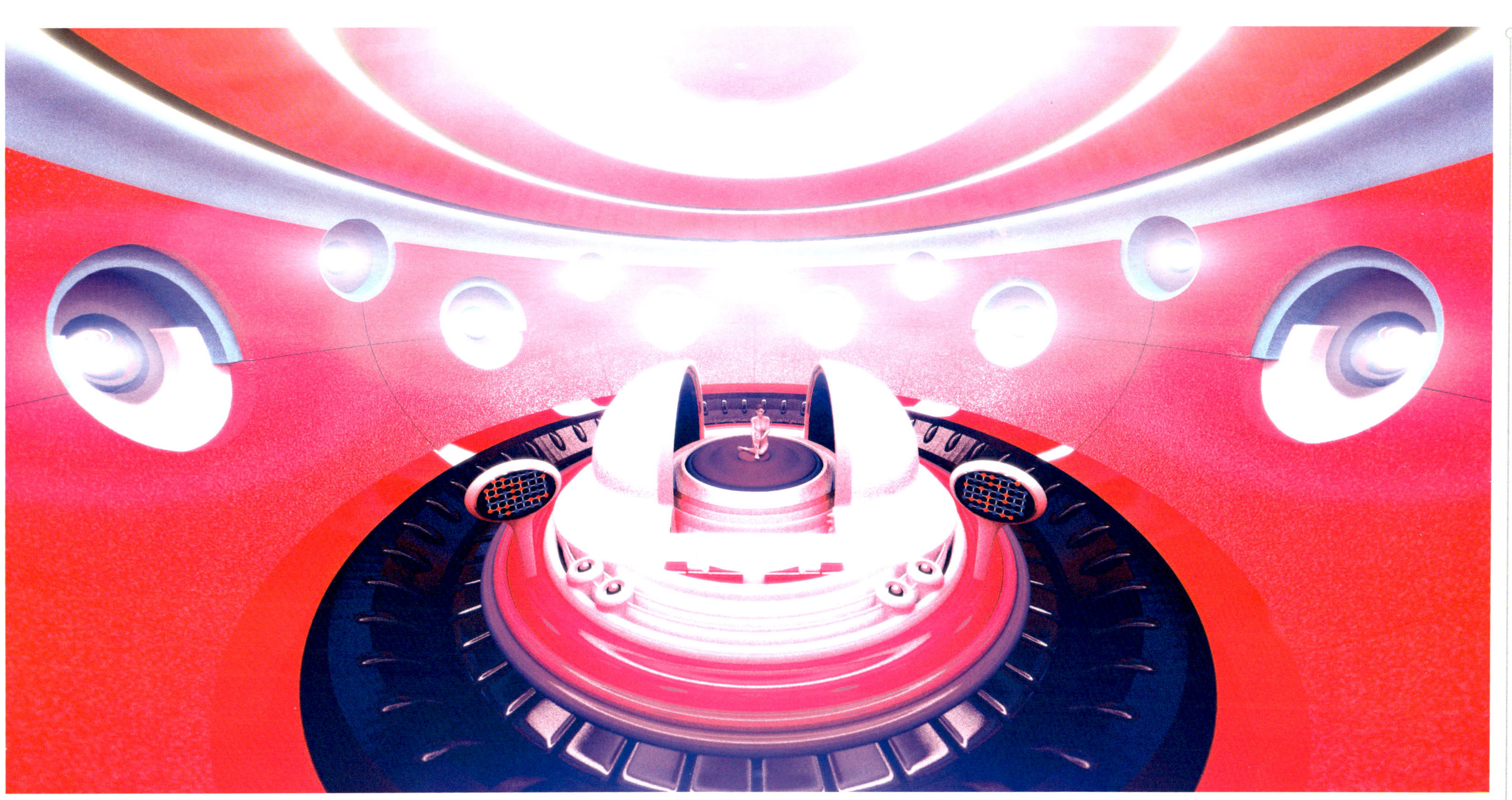

- SOIN -
3000 x 1500 pixels

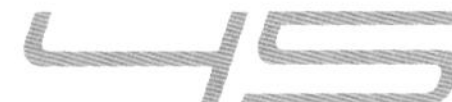

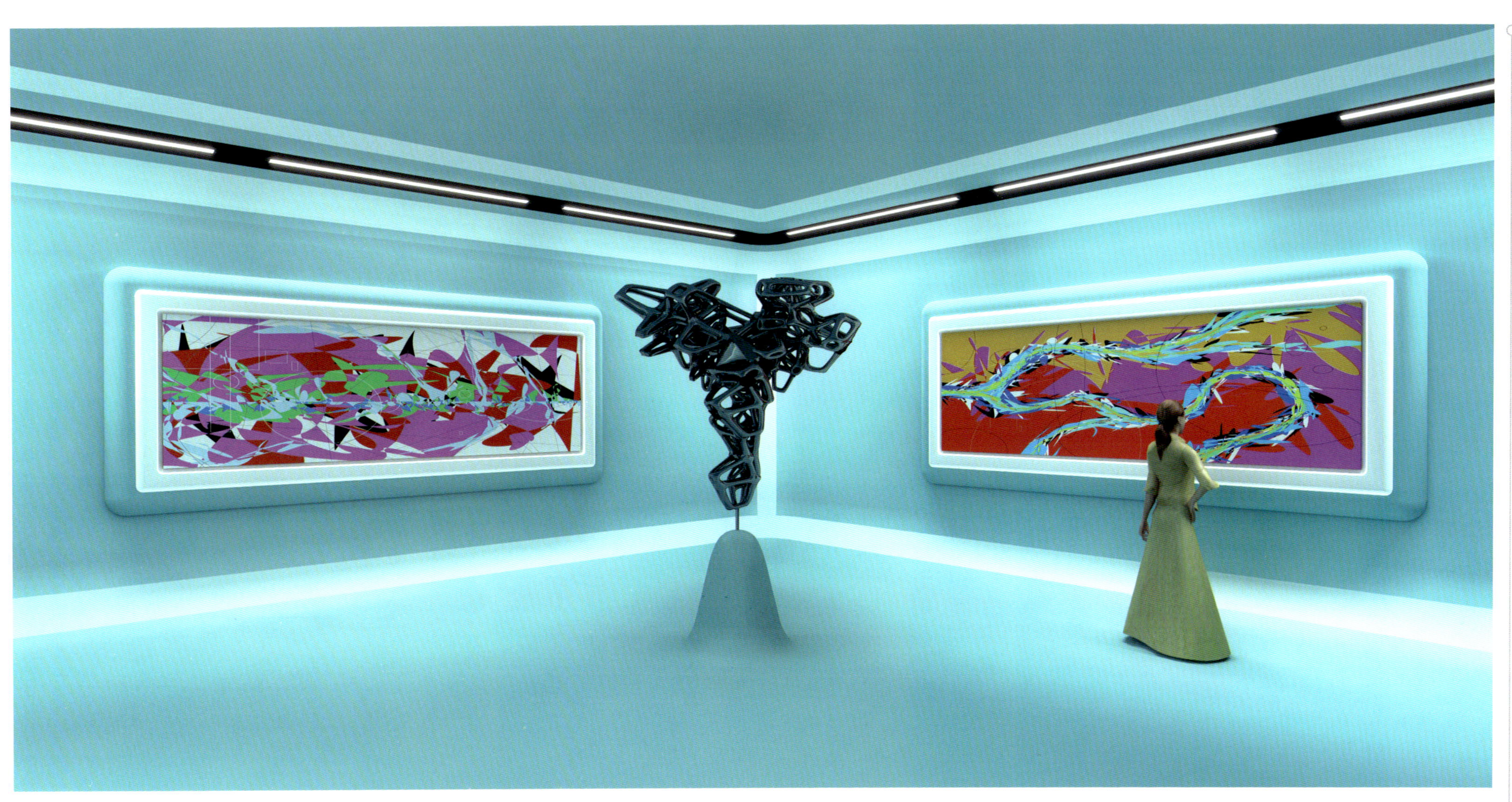

BLUE
3000 x 1500 pixels

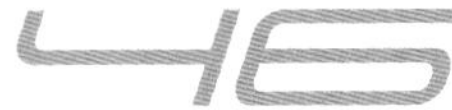

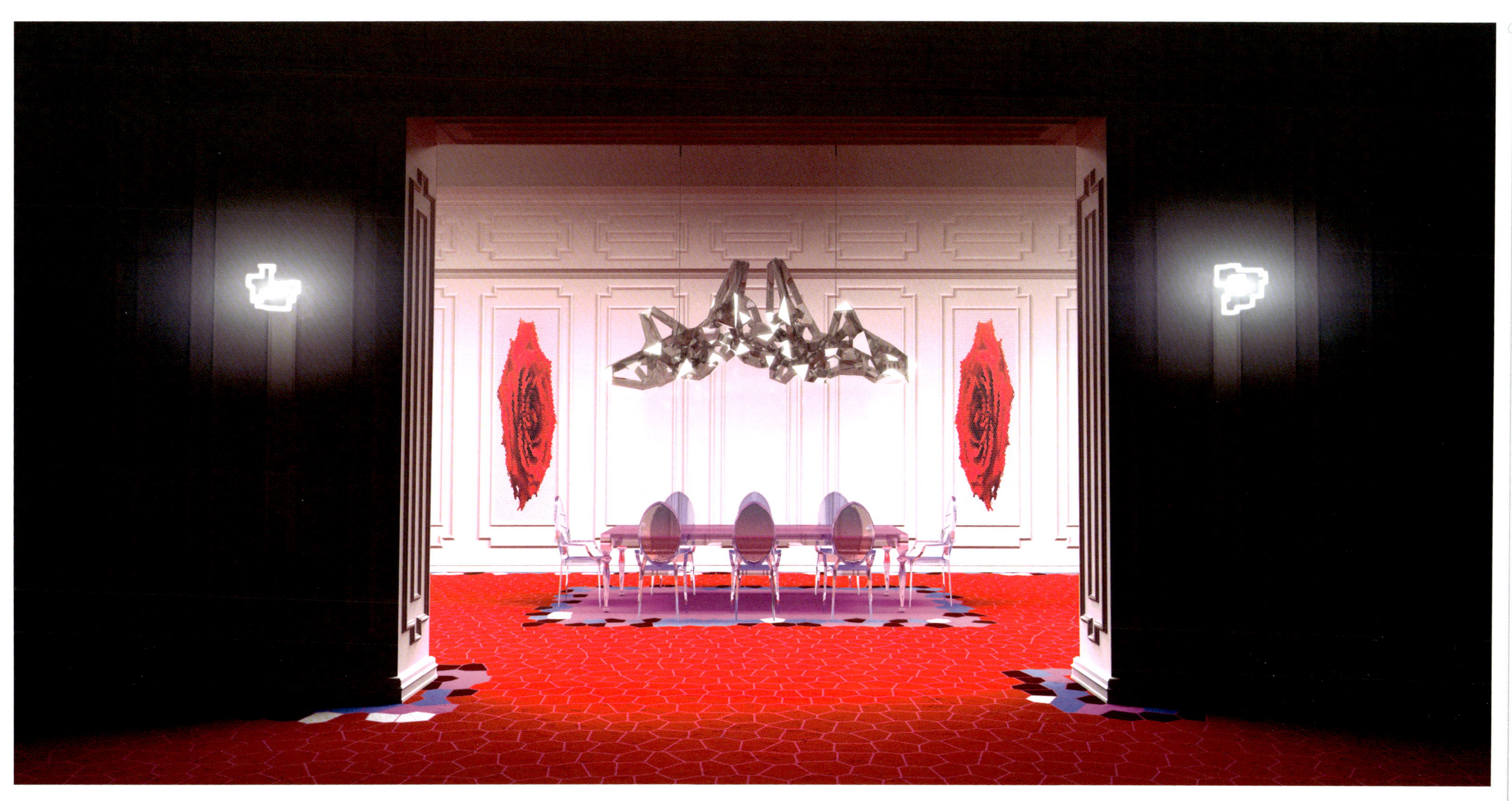

CALSEC PROSCOV
3000 x 1500 pixels

47

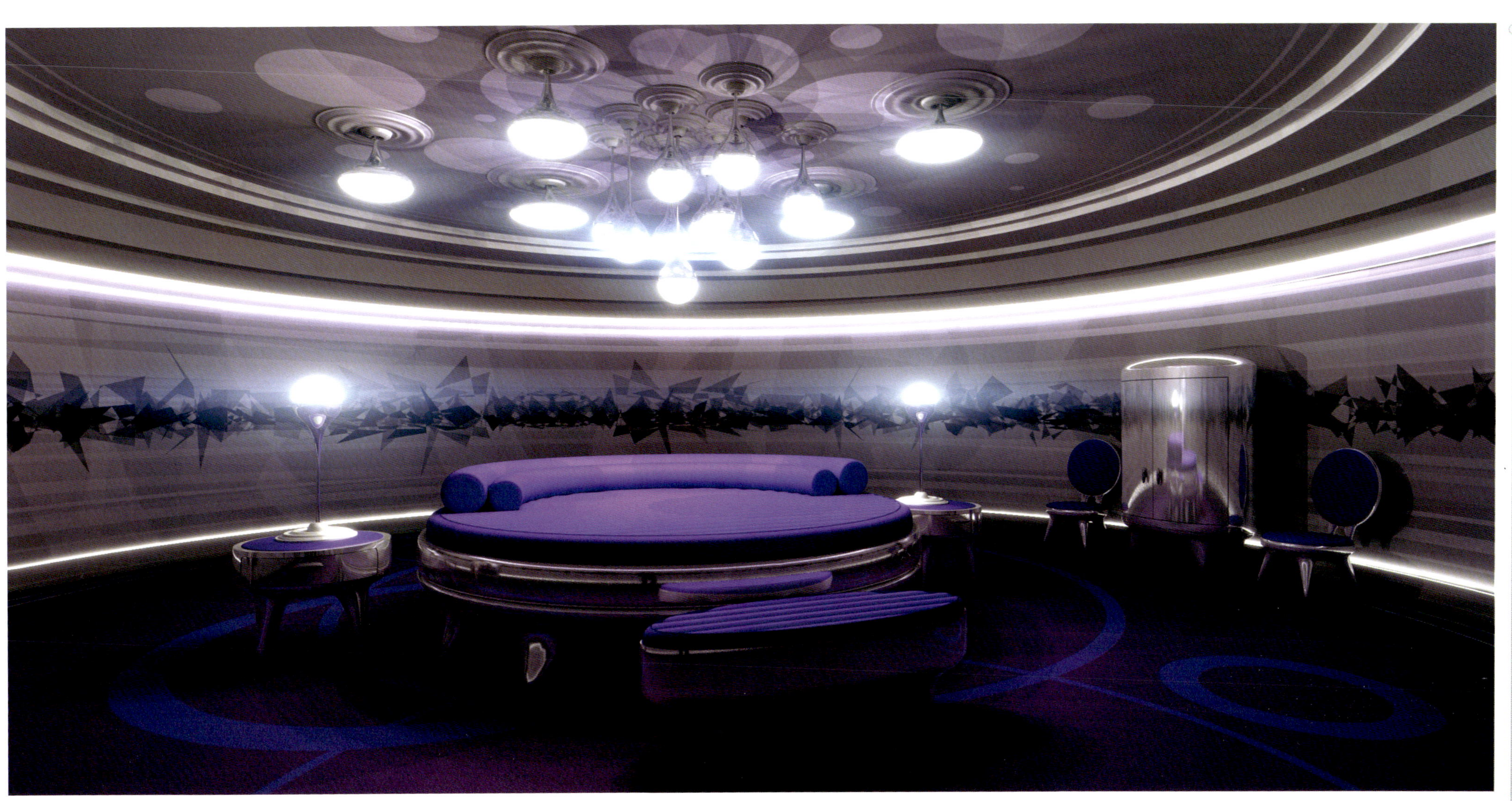

REST
3000 x 1500 pixels

48

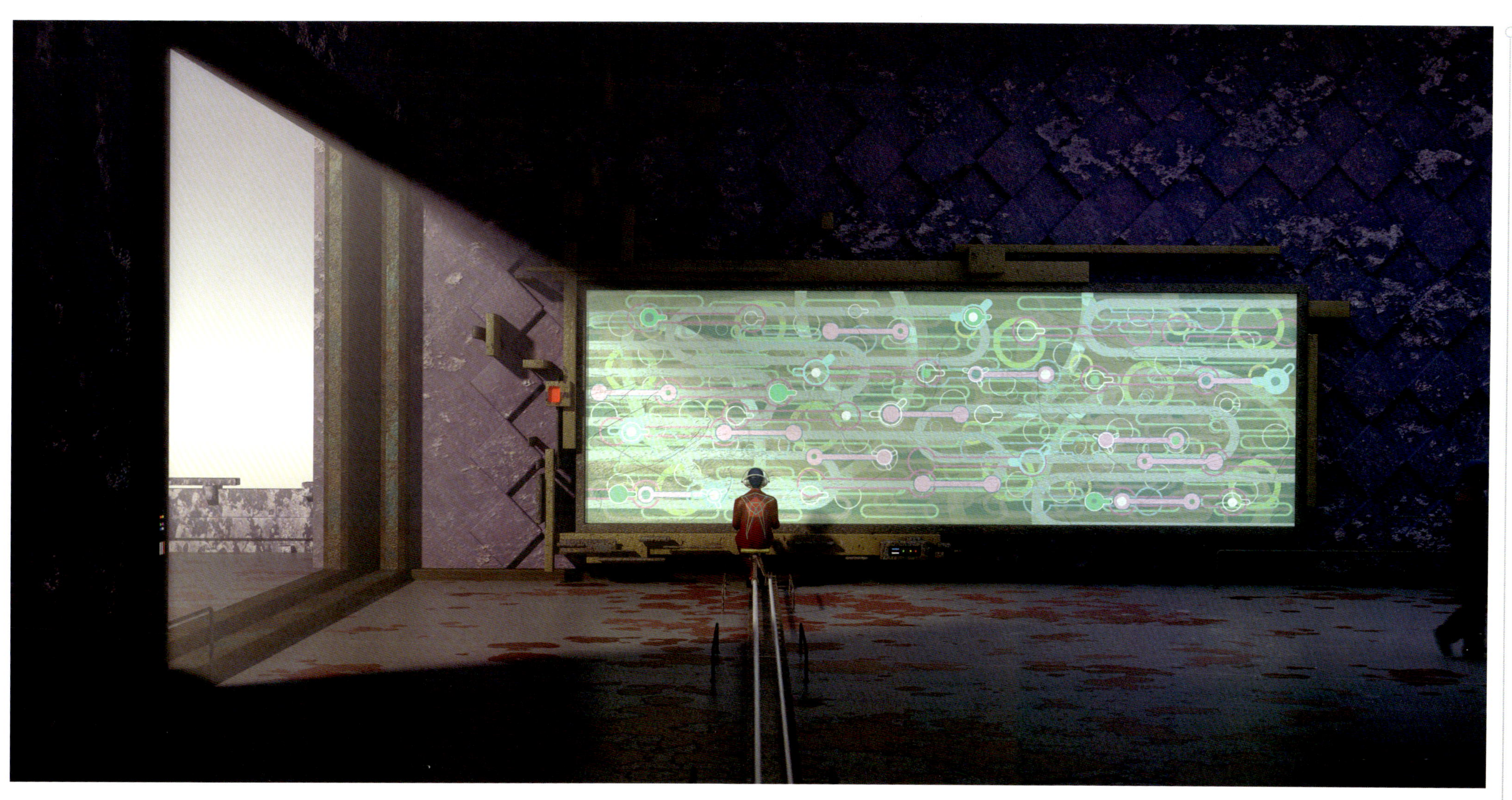

LEA GENTRELICOM
3000 x 1500 pixels

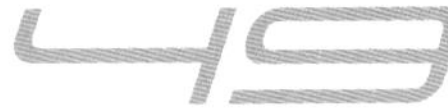

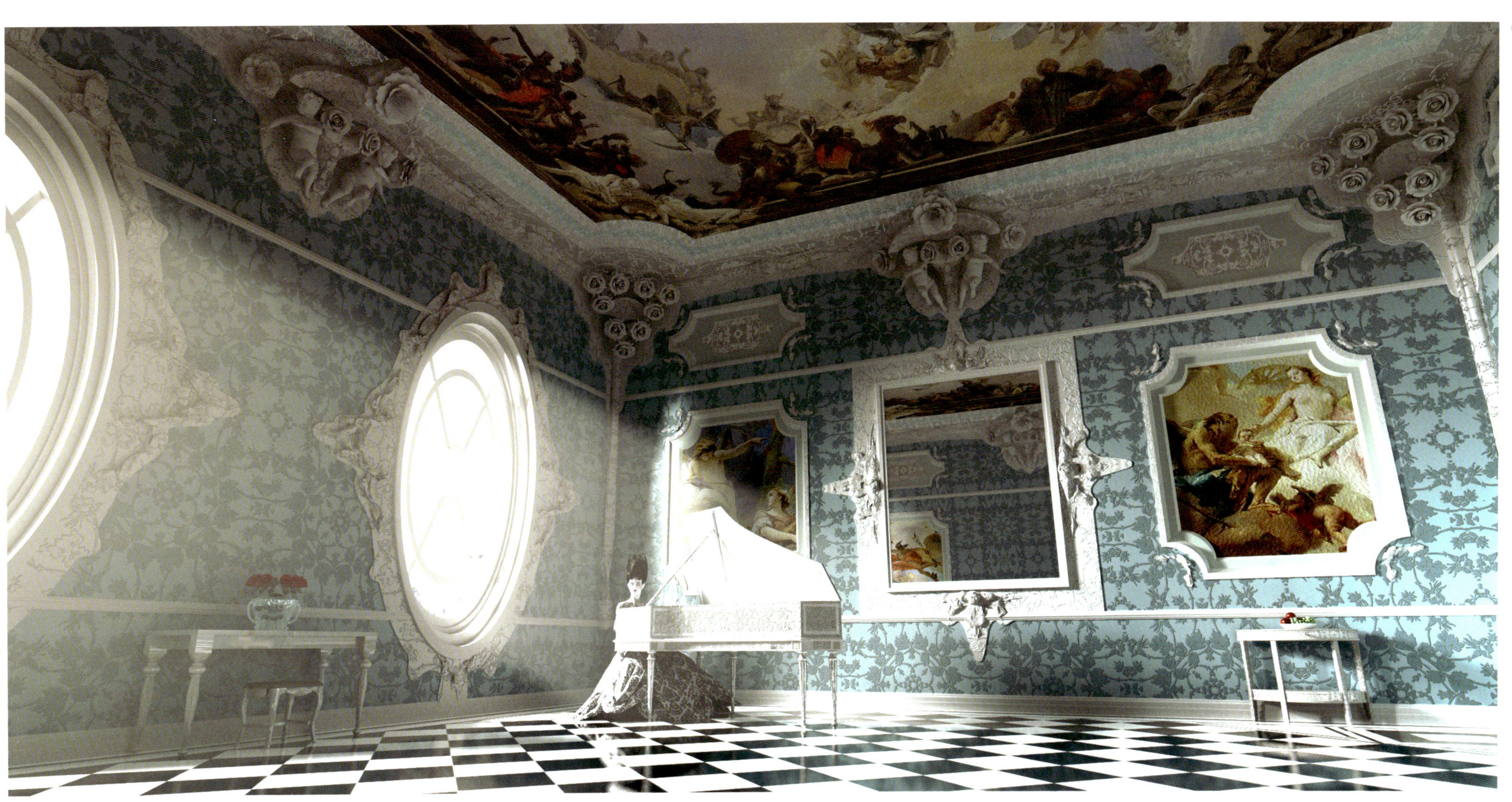
8AM SUNDAY
3000 x 1500 pixels
SEÁN HARGREAVES : PLACES

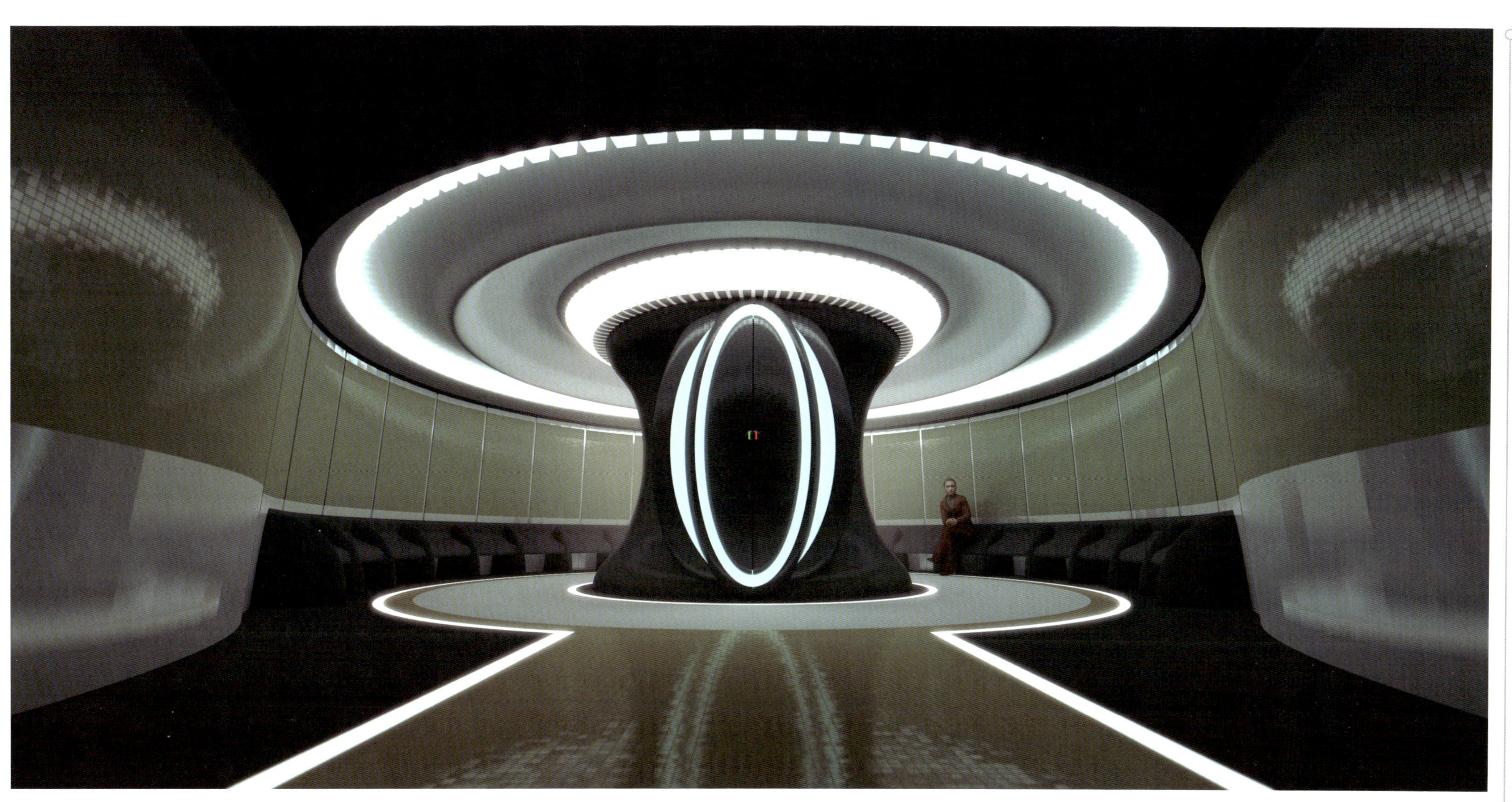

INTERNAL TRANSFER
4000 x 2000 pixels

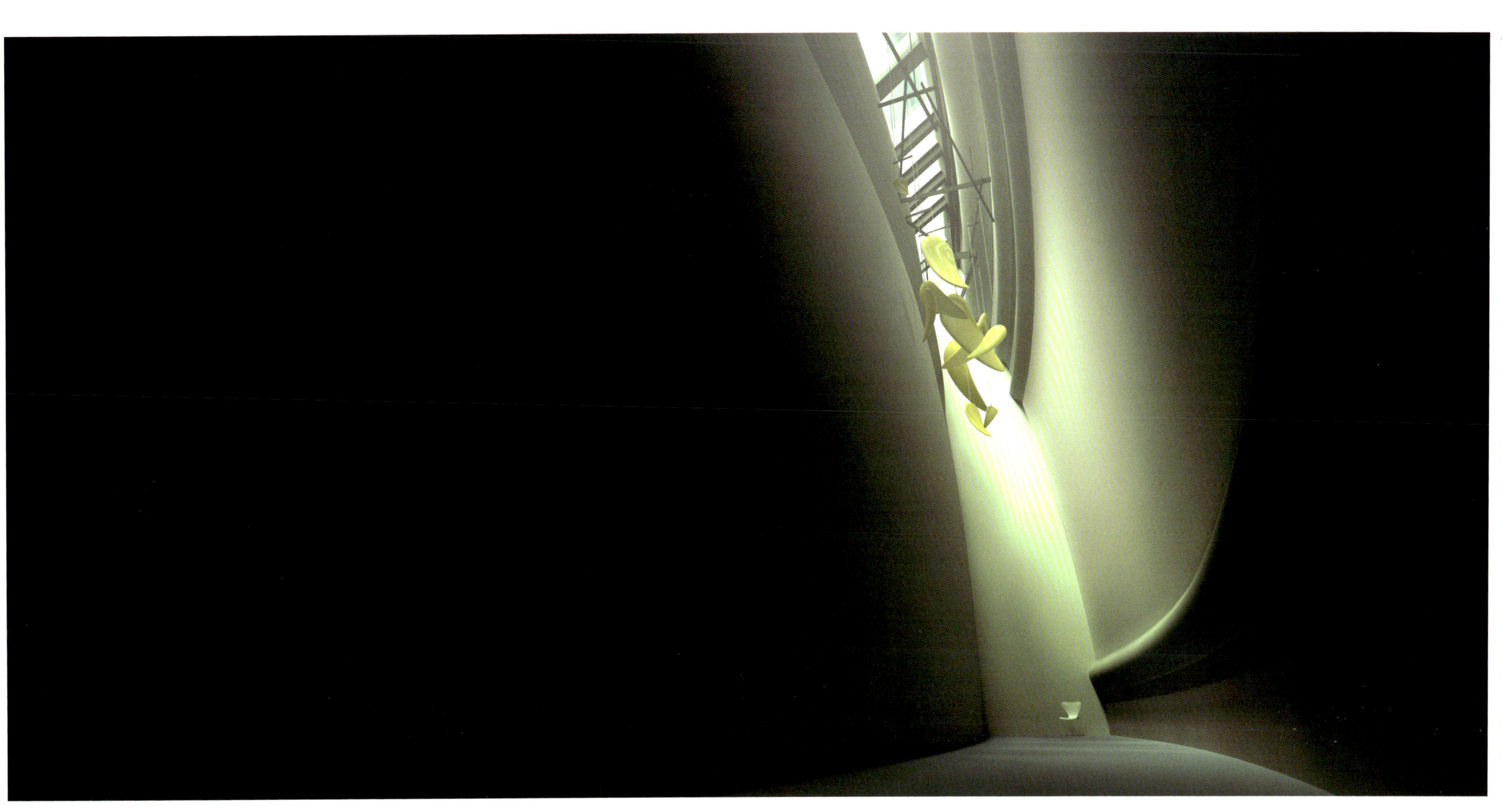

HALLWAY
4000 x 2000 pixels

52

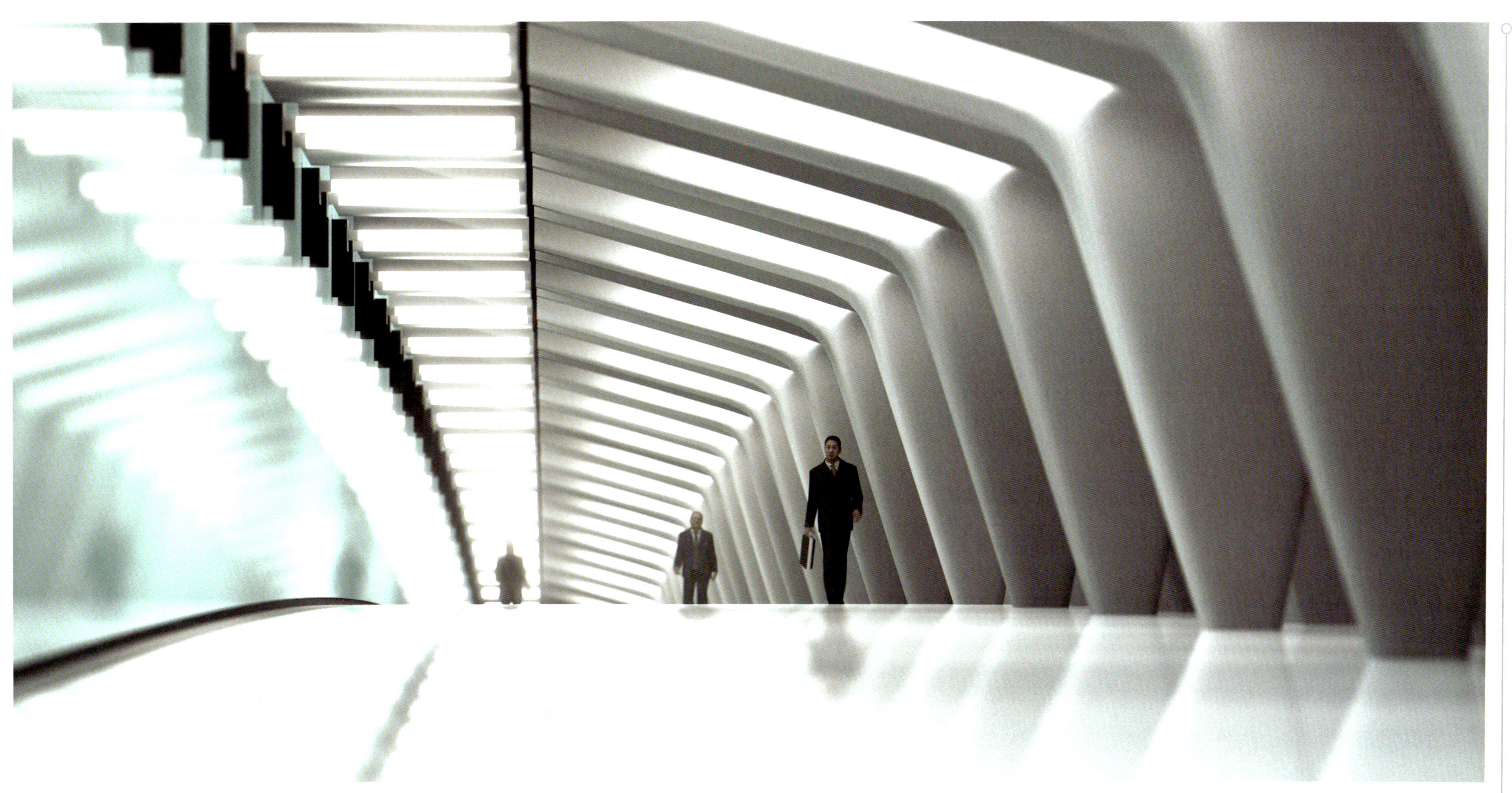

TRESMEN
4000 x 2000 pixels

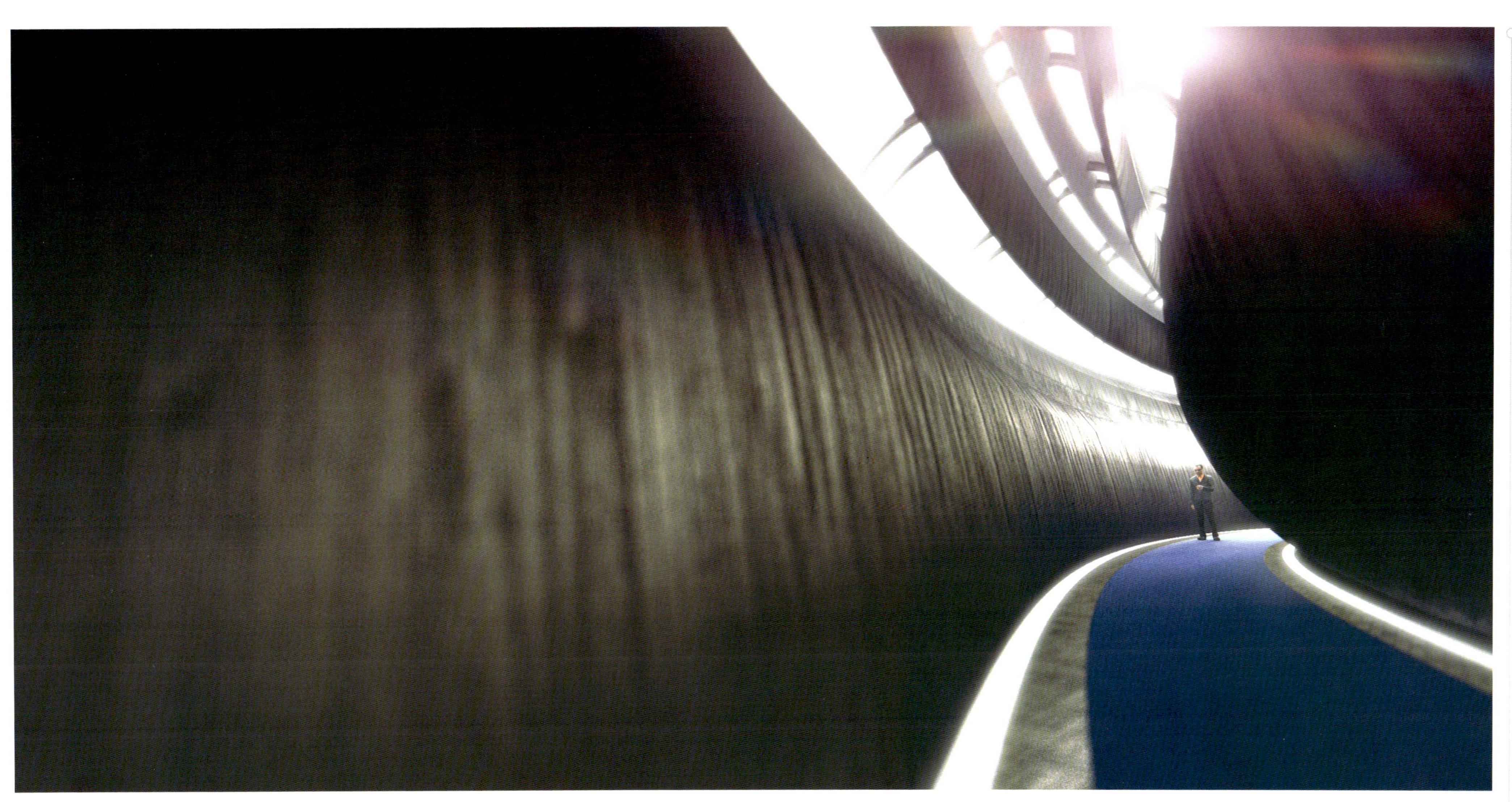

TIME ENOUGH

3000 x 1500 pixels

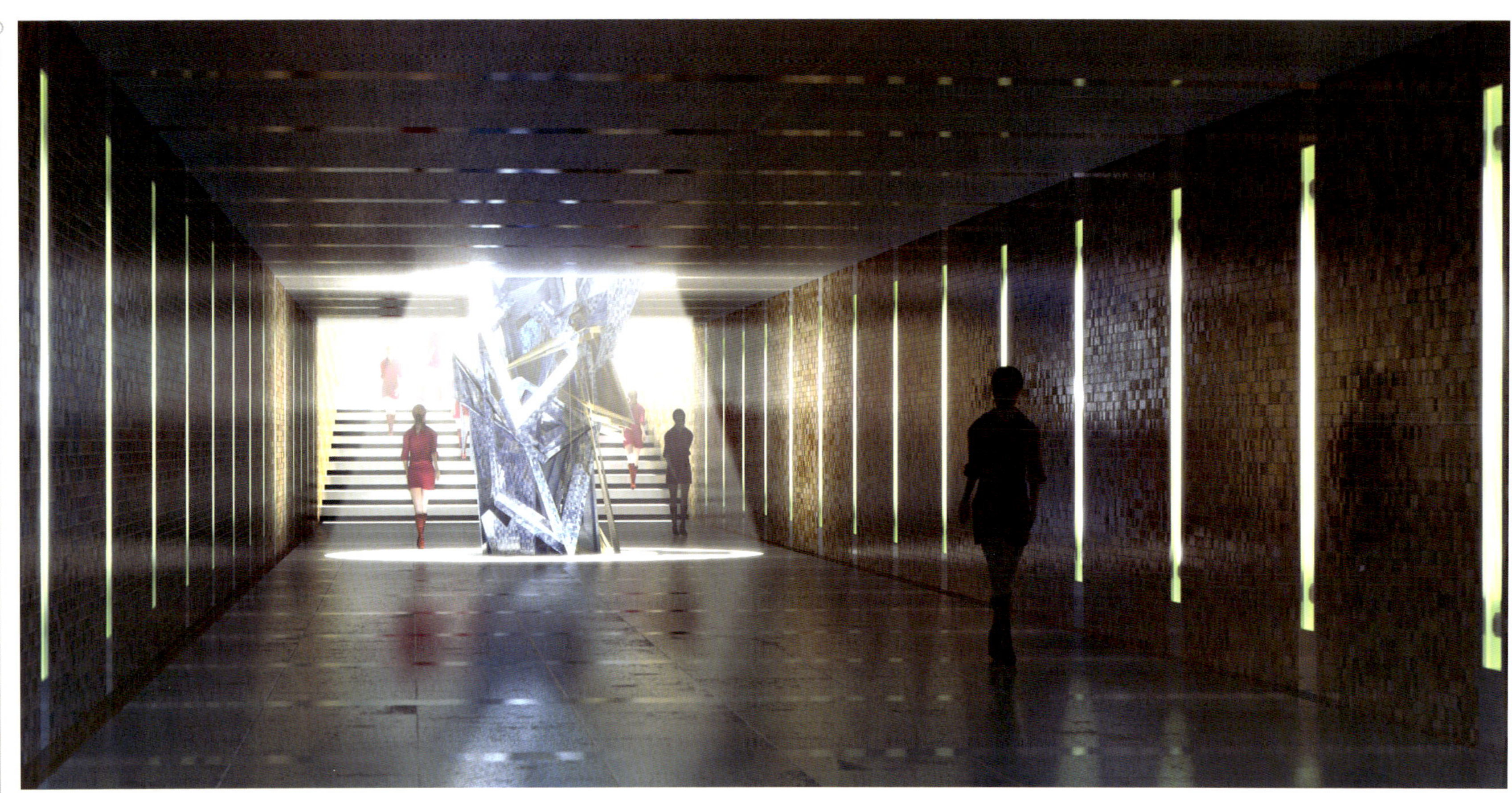

54

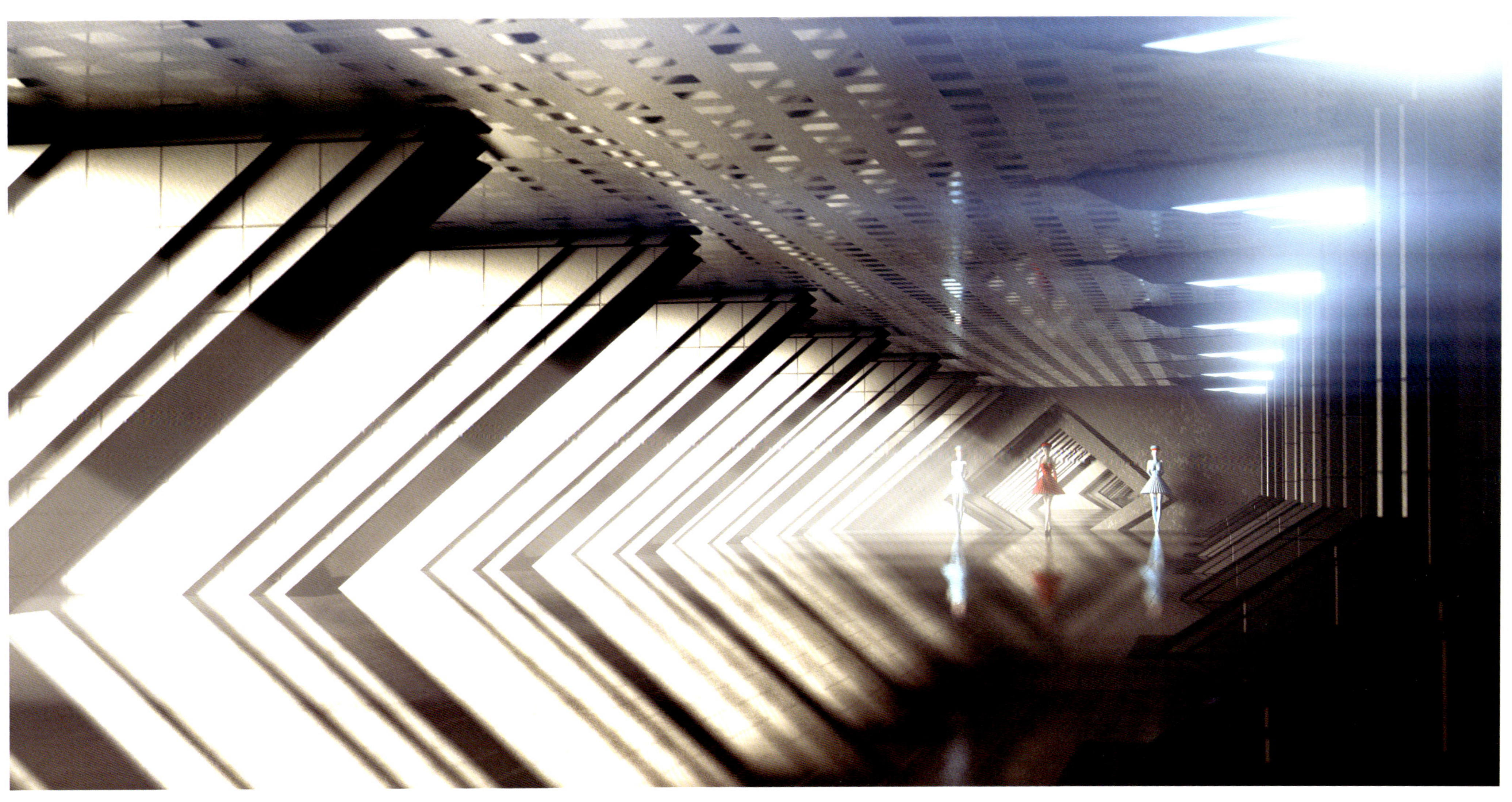
55
OFFICE (3)
3000 x 1500 pixels
SEÁN HARGREAVES : PLACES

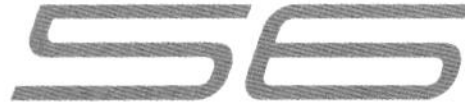

An underground corridor. Rusted, aged, strange sounds in the background. It sits just below the surface, and you can see a little dapple of green through the skylight. The machine at the end is part of a door-opening system of hidden gears. One needs a type of handle that rotates the mechanism to open the door. Inside the diamond-shaped window above the mechanism, there is the face of a boy peeking through.

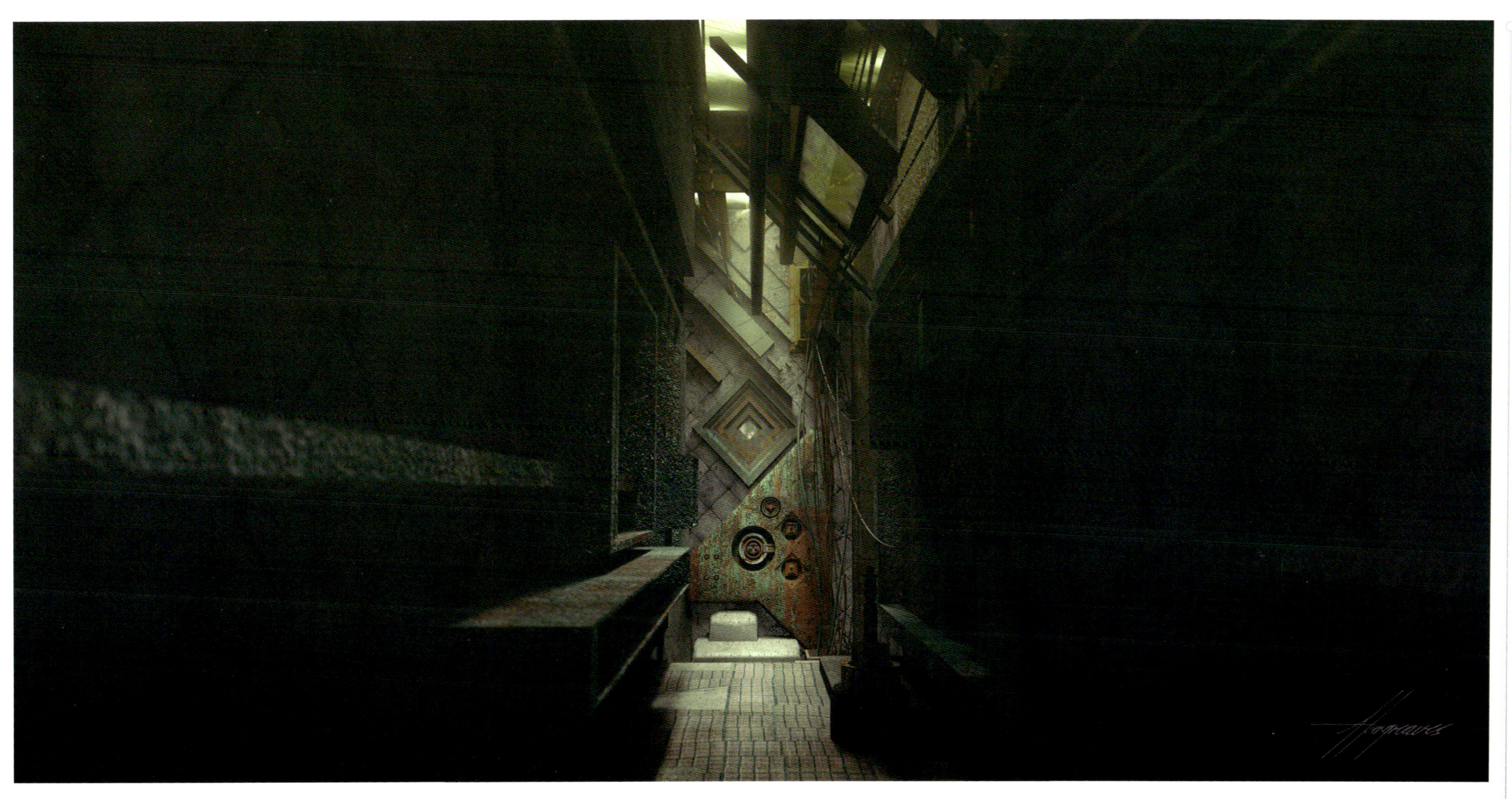

CARTHAACTUM
3000 x 1500 pixels

57

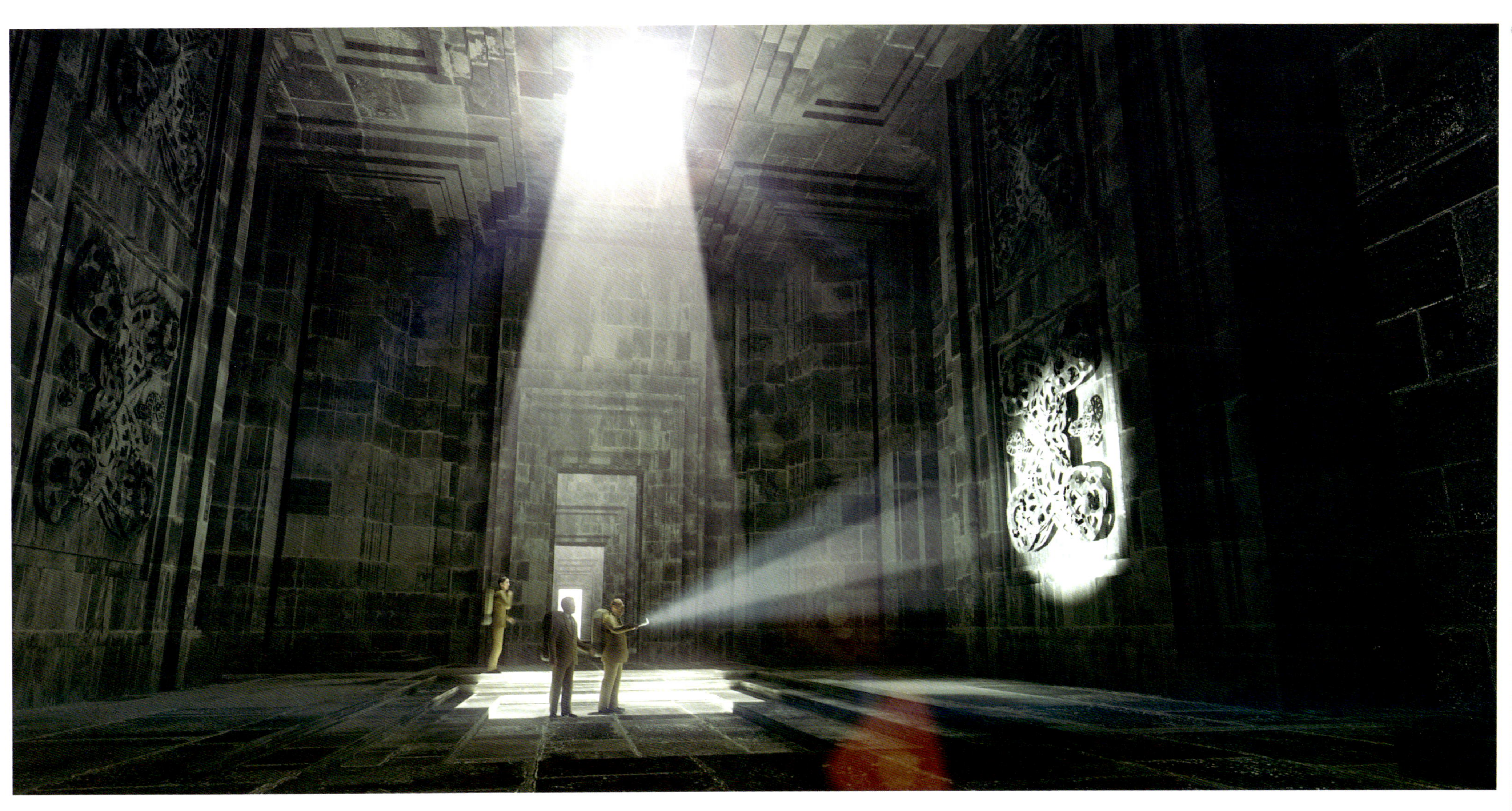

WALL
3000 x 1500 pixels

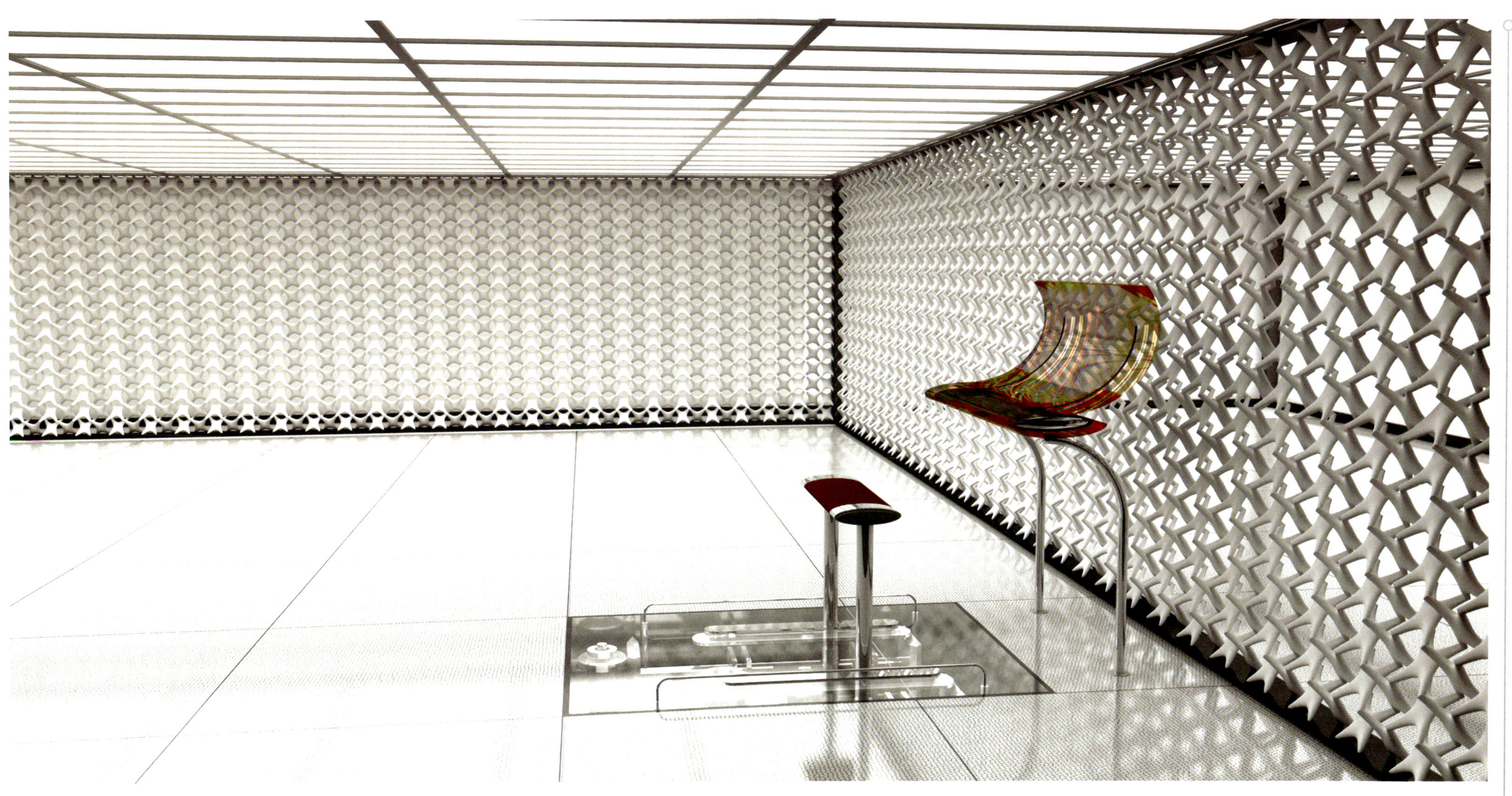

ACRYLIC KEYBOARD
3000 x 1500 pixels

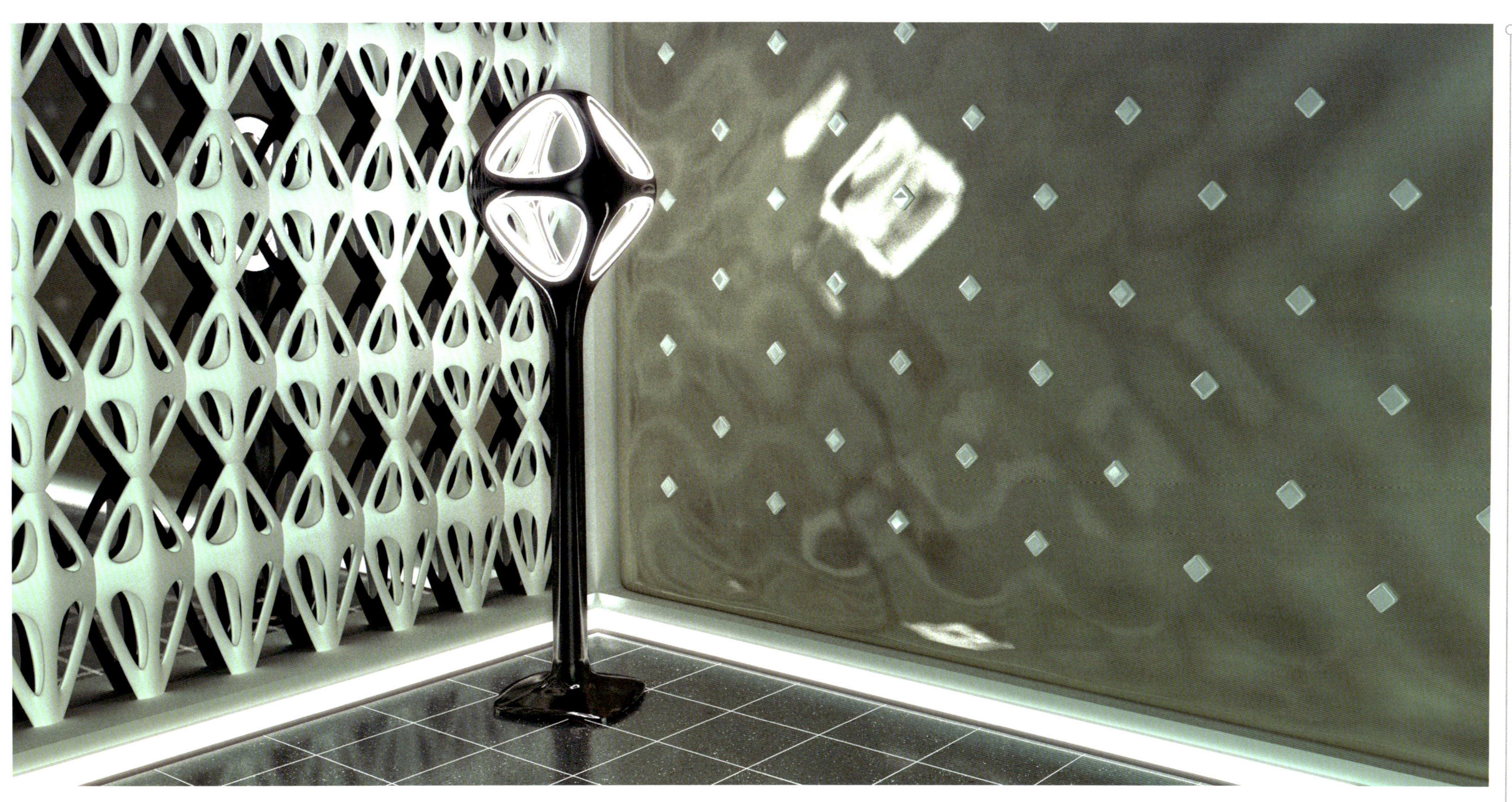

LAMP
3000 x 1500 pixels

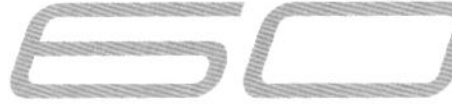

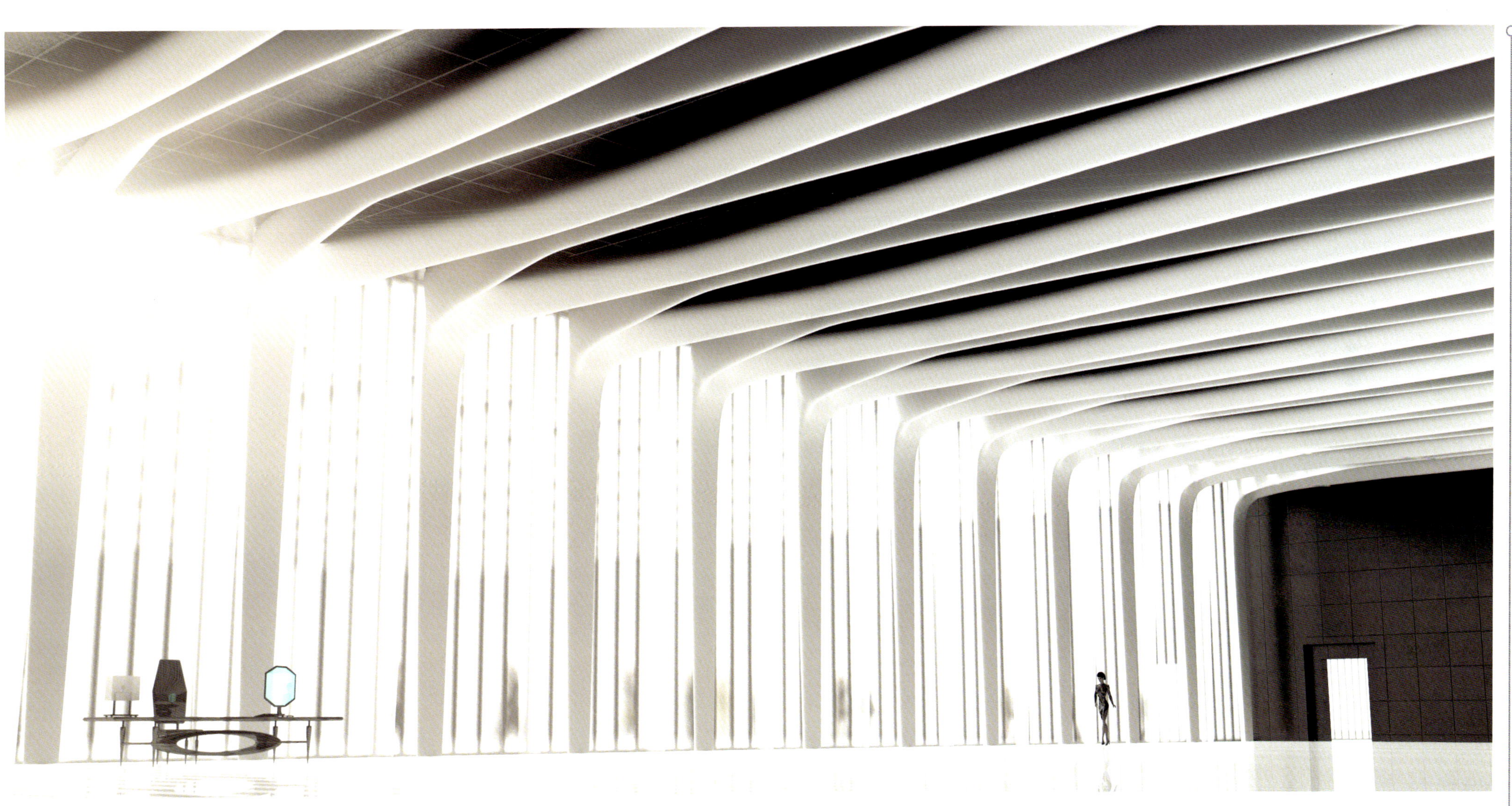

OFFICE

3000 x 1500 pixels

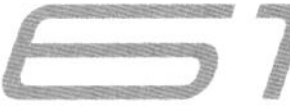

The silence of an empty room. Pull one of the metal-framed chairs from under the table and you can hear the high-pitched scraping sound as the legs move across the tile. The glass of the table and chairs create an extreme refraction of the surfaces beyond when viewed through the glass. The walls are faceted mirrors, creating an infinity effect on the eye.

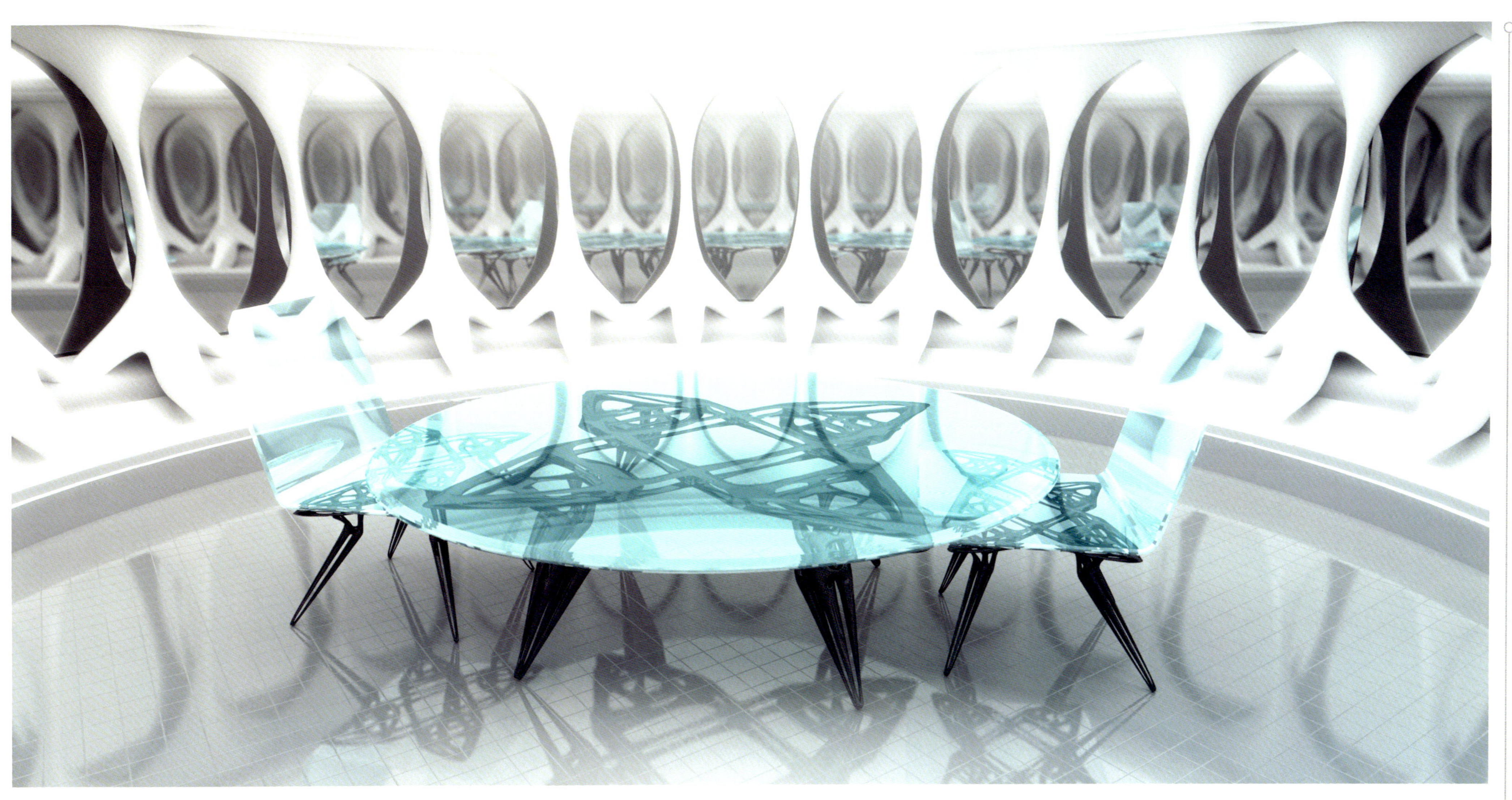

TABLE AND CHAIRS IN A ROOM
3000 x 1500 pixels

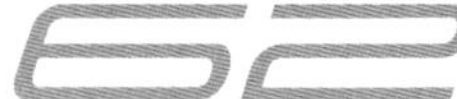

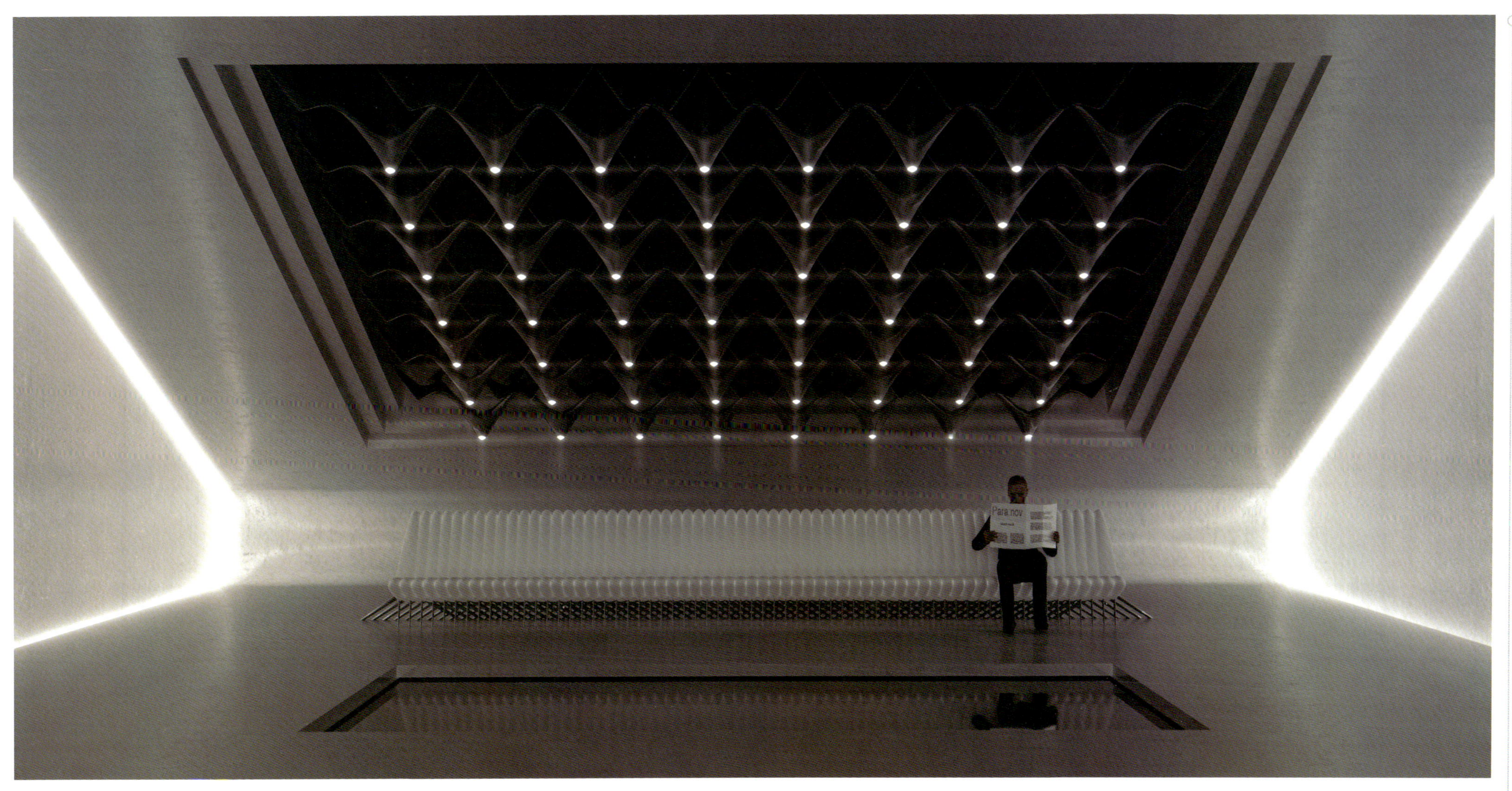

VARTRELIS 5
3000 x 1500 pixels

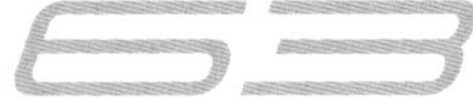

A simple gallery. Abstract works by Frances adorn the walls. As one steps closer, the art vibrates, shimmers. Step even closer and the work comes alive, animating itself out from the frame.

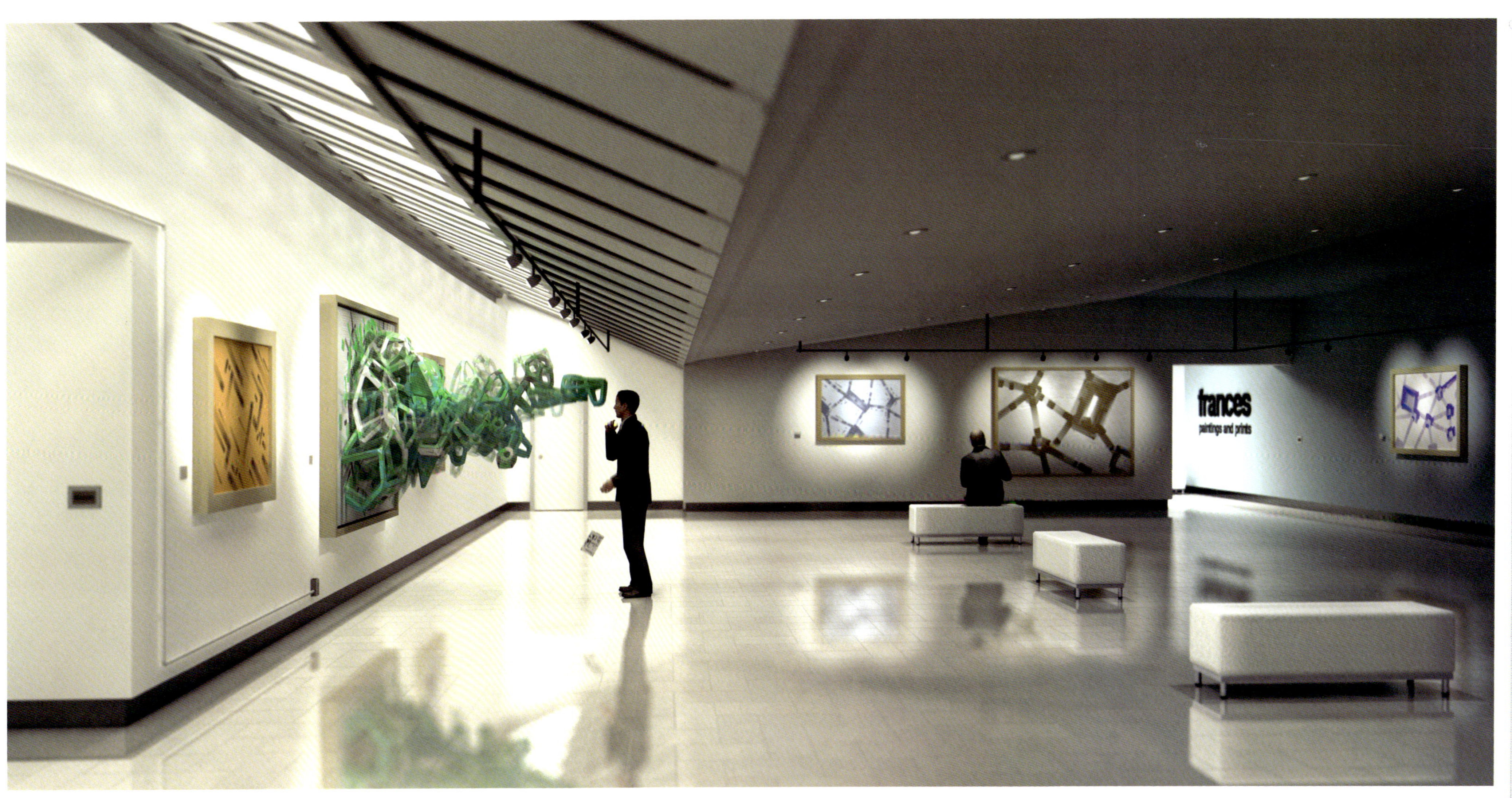

NAES

3000 x 1500 pixels

64

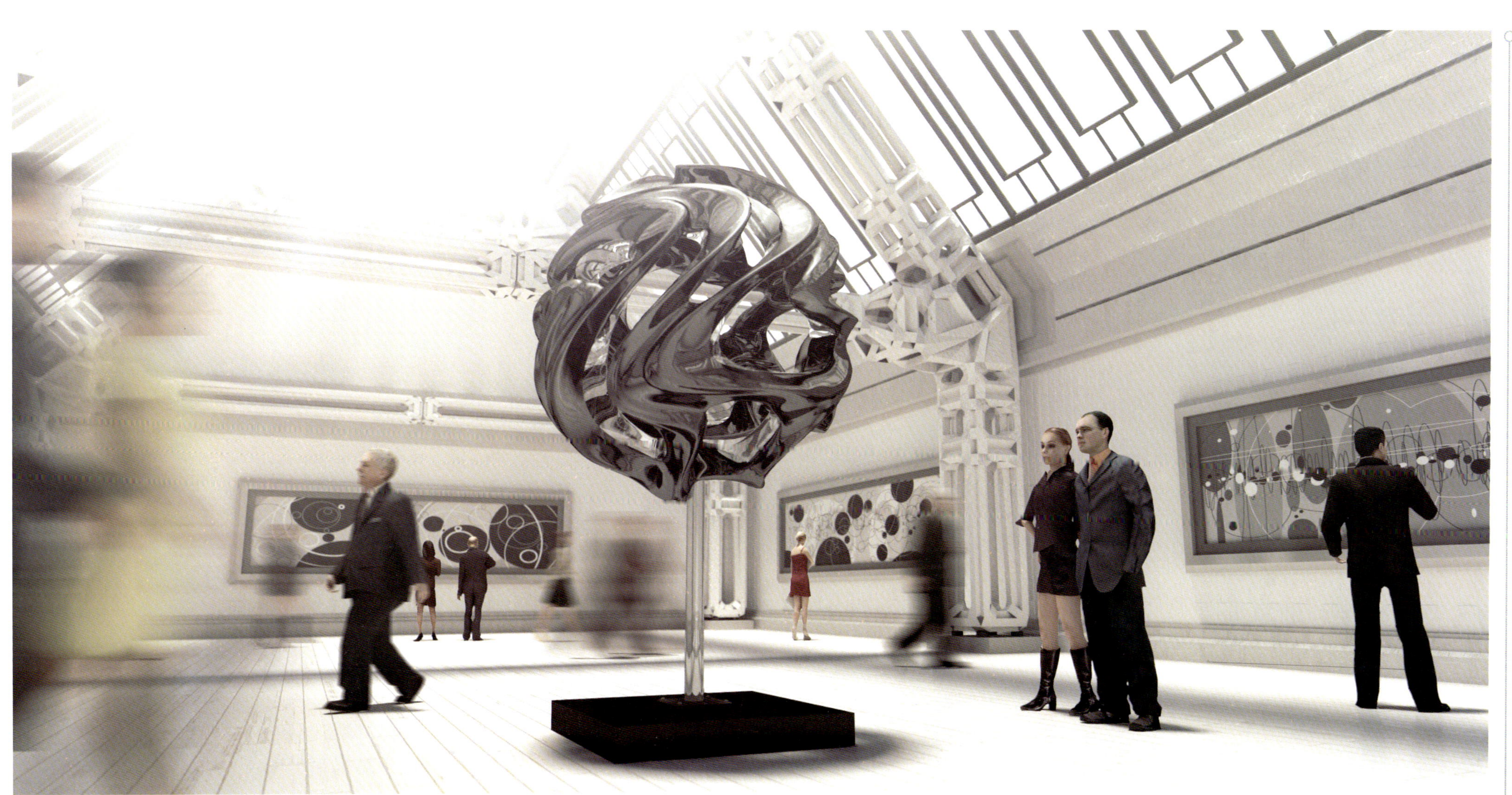

SCULPTURE
3000 x 1500 pixels
SEÁN HARGREAVES : PLACES

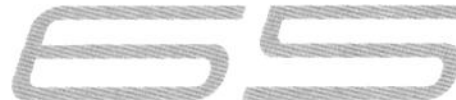

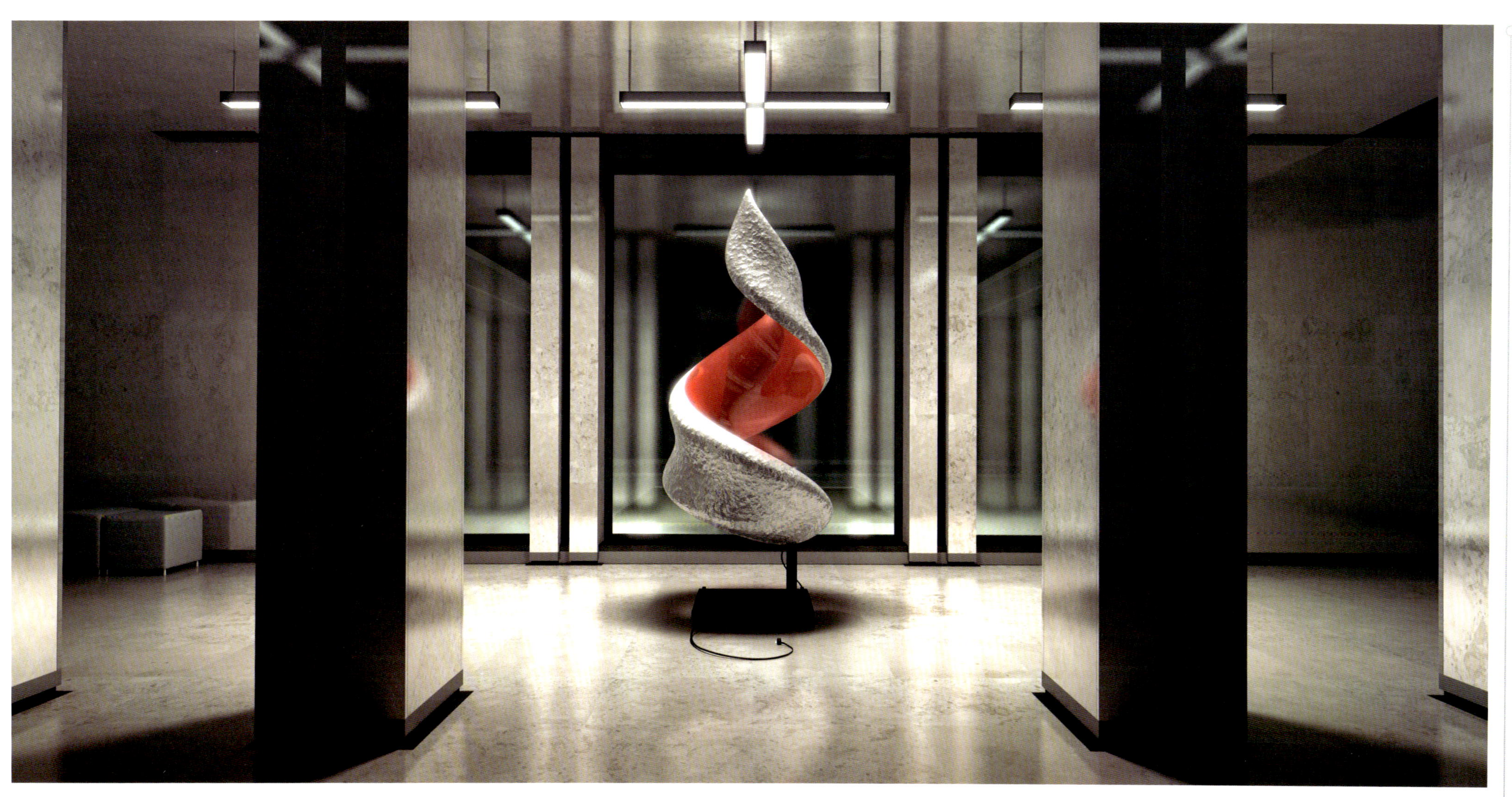

ENTER THROUGH THE LOBBY
AND SIT ON THE LEFT
4000 x 2000 pixels

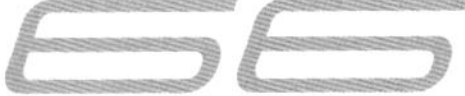

When I was young my father began the building of a large remote-controlled plane. The wings, which were 4' long, were made of a wooden frame and covered in a shrink-wrapped opaque plastic that was as tight as a drum. Here I've presented an art piece made of a similar technique. The surface is delicate and very easy to puncture, and it has an almost translucent quality.

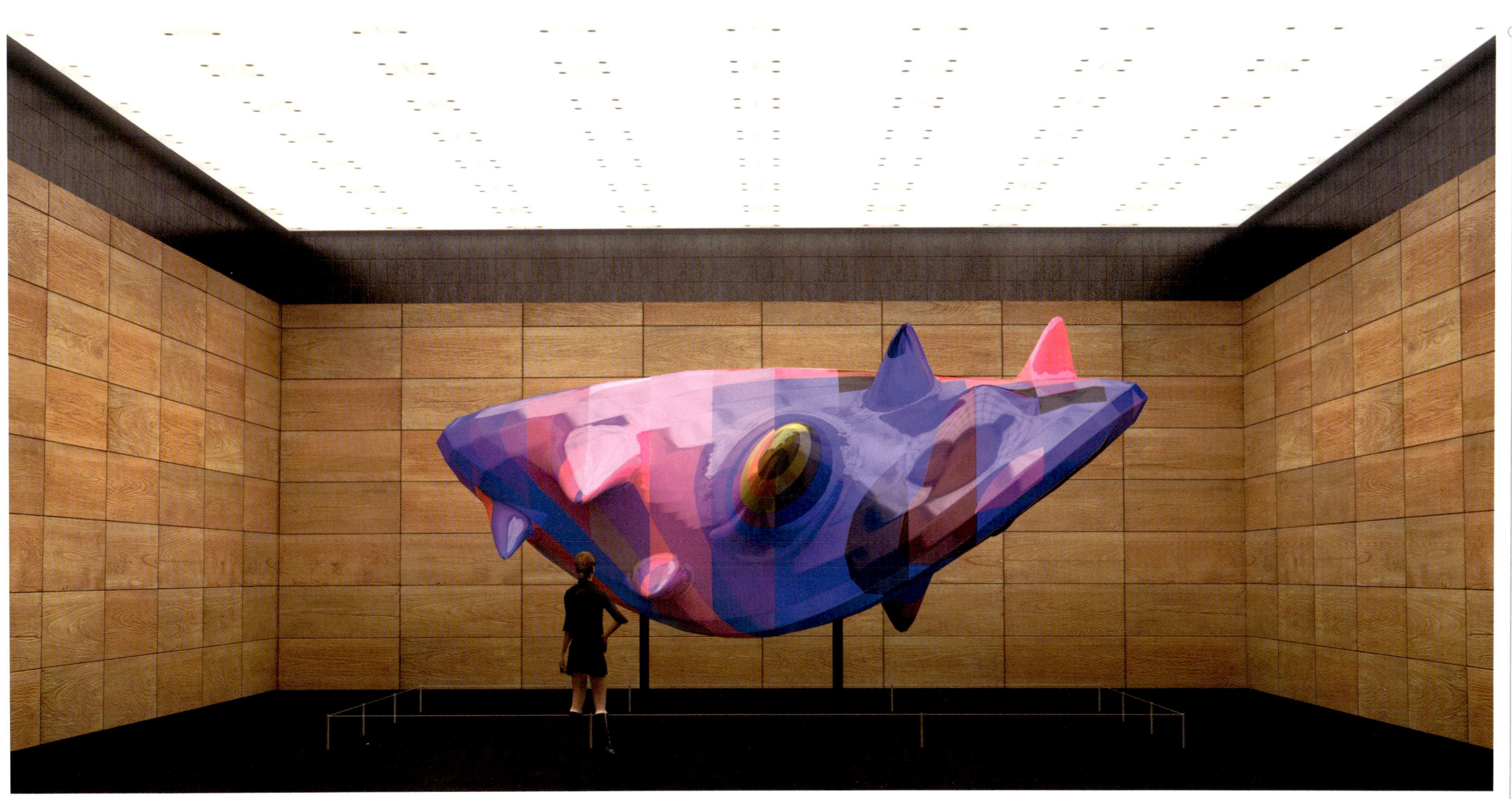

PRELLEM
4000 x 2000 pixels

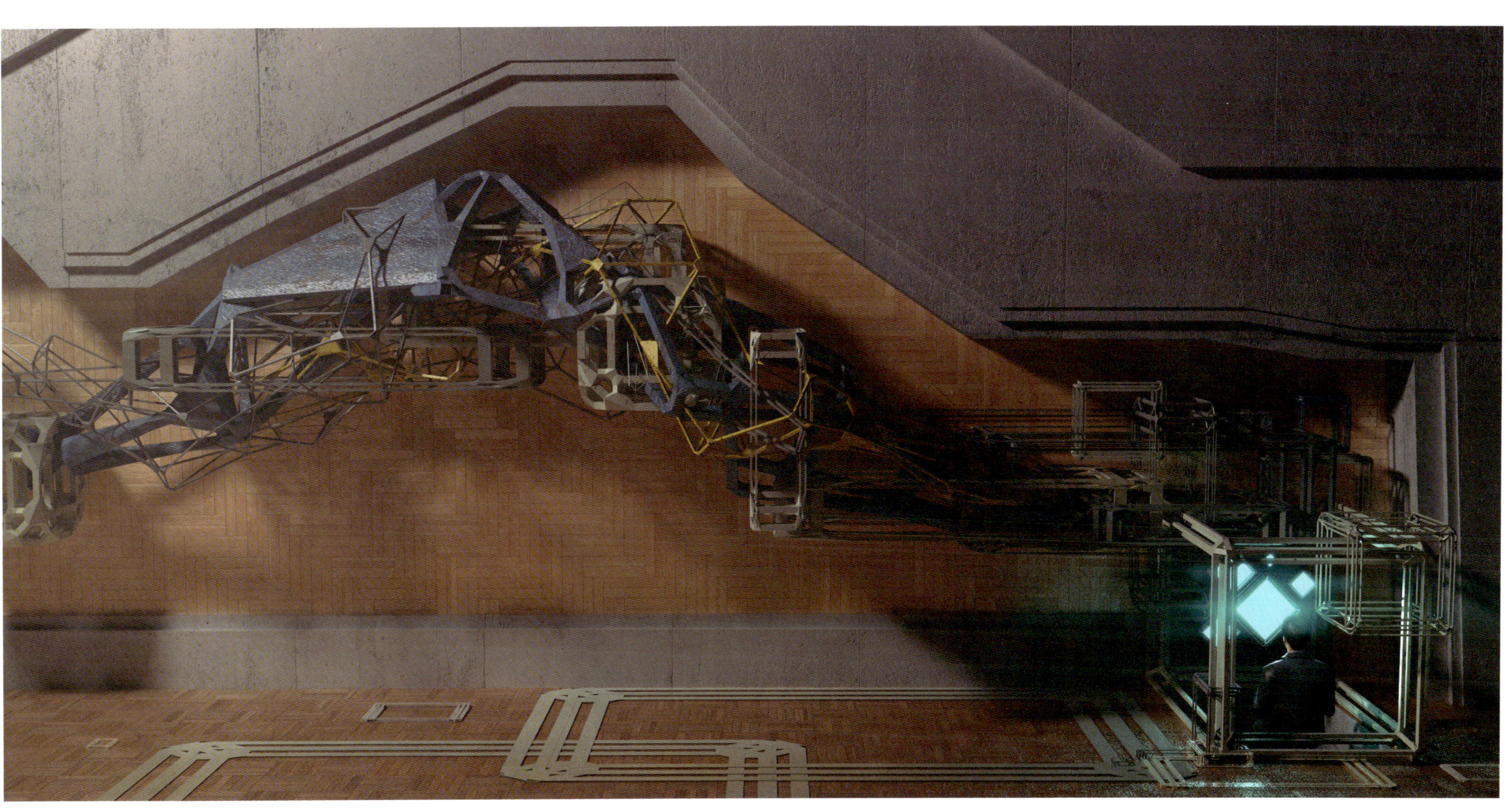

WETH 0--
3000 x 1500 pixels

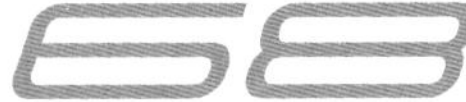

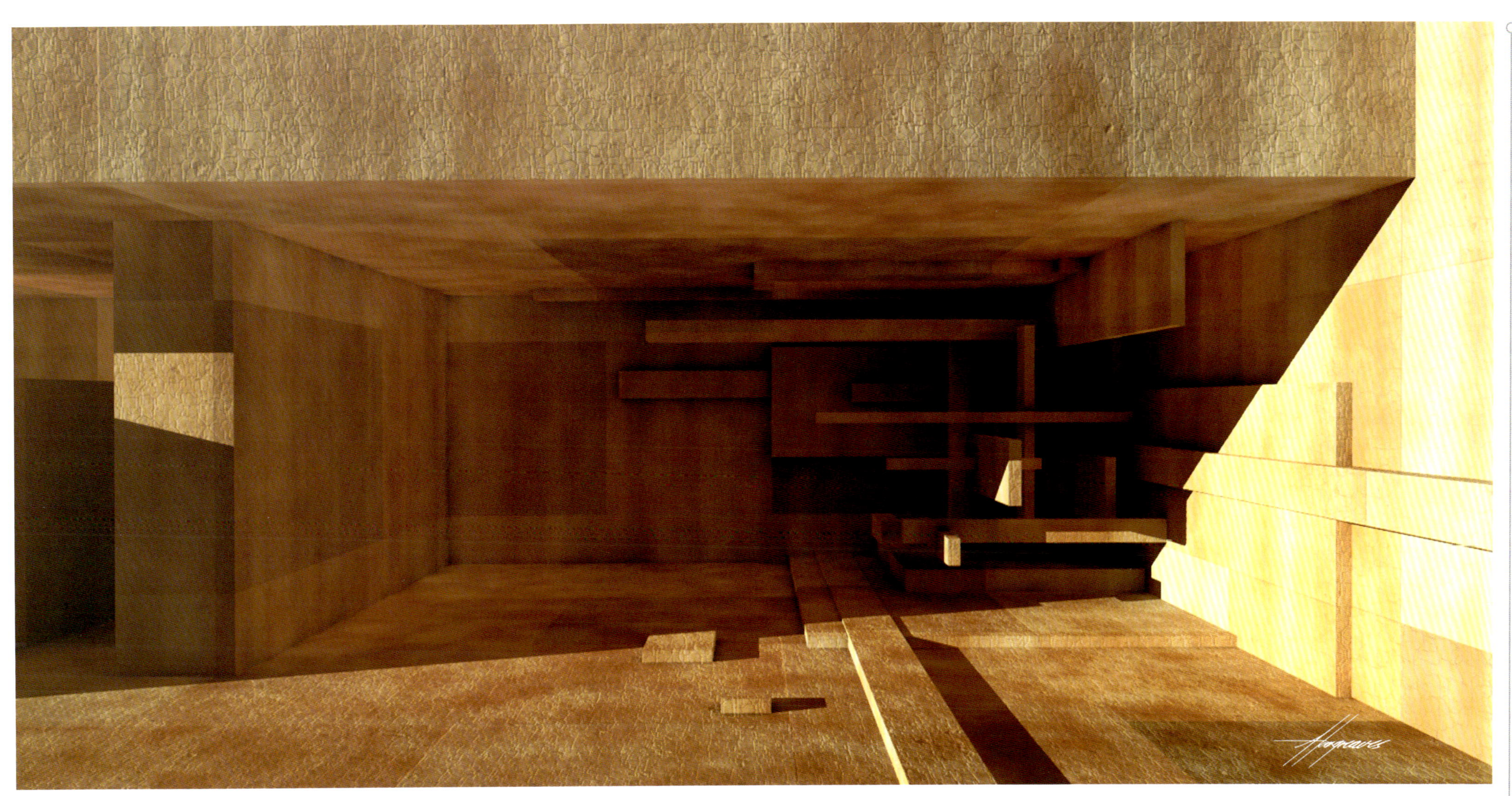

DESERT HOME

3000 x 1500 pixels

69

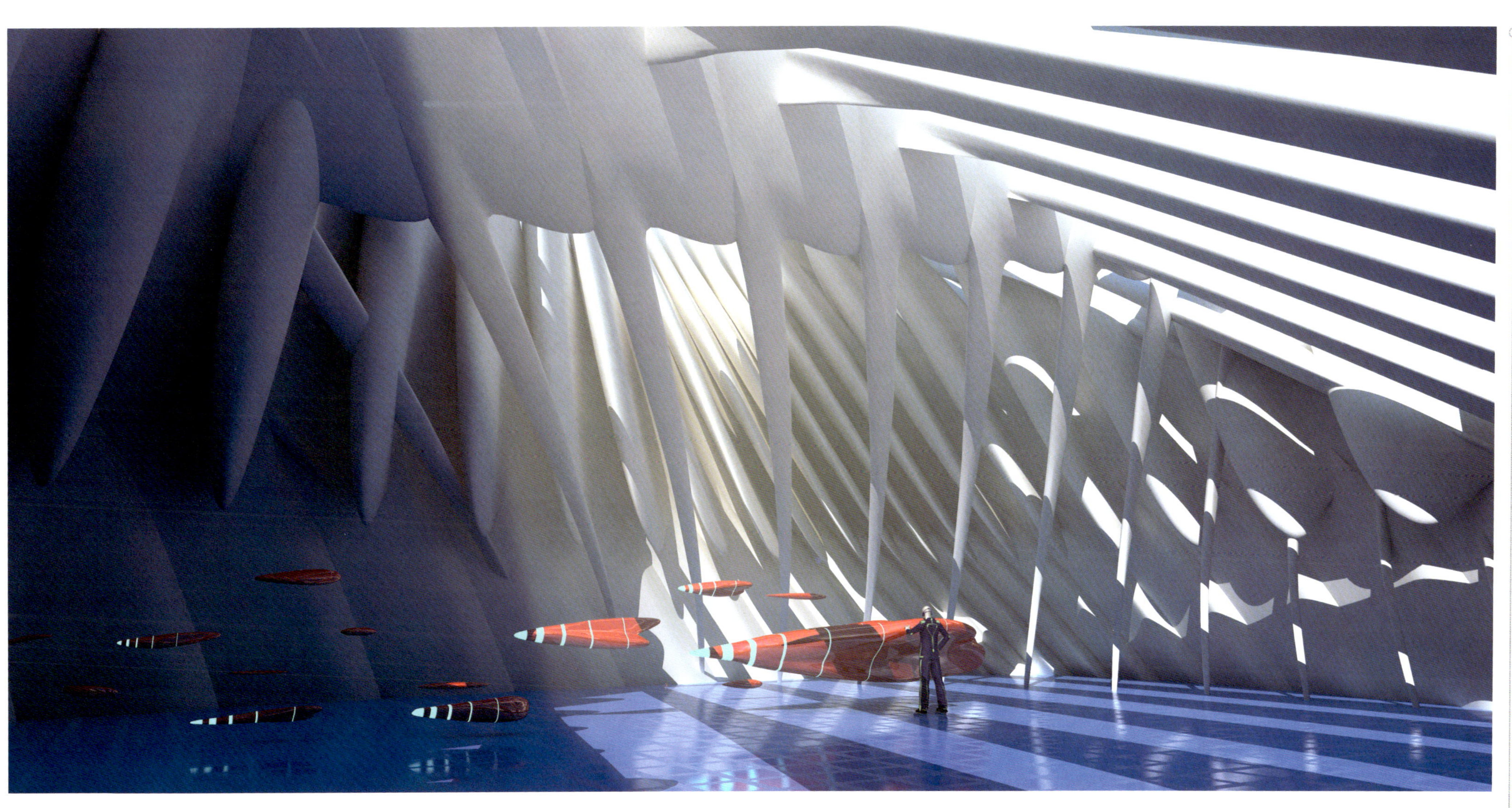

PARALLAX VENTRIFORM
3000 x 1500 pixels

70

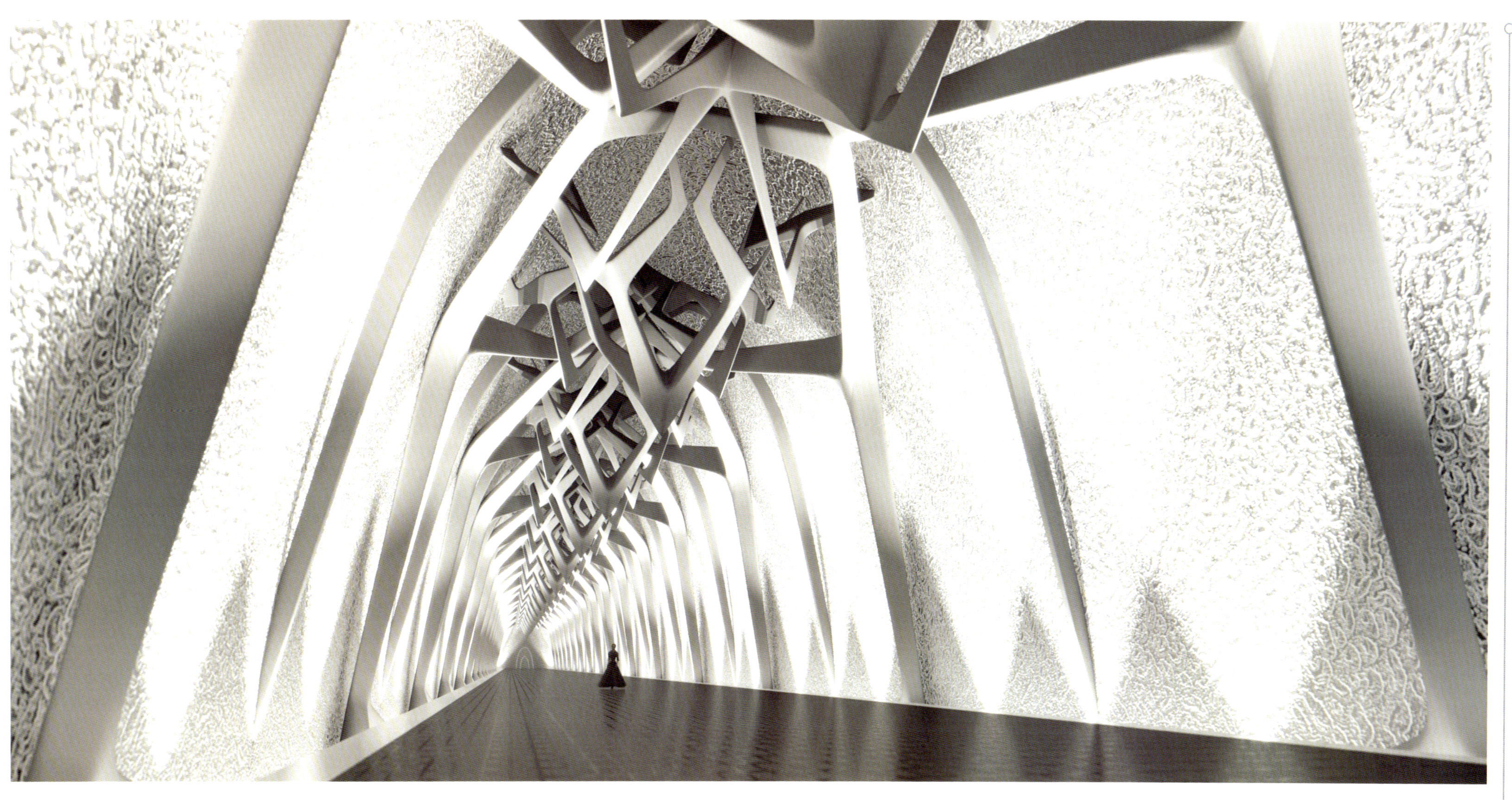

SPINAL CORRIDOR
3000 x 1500 pixels

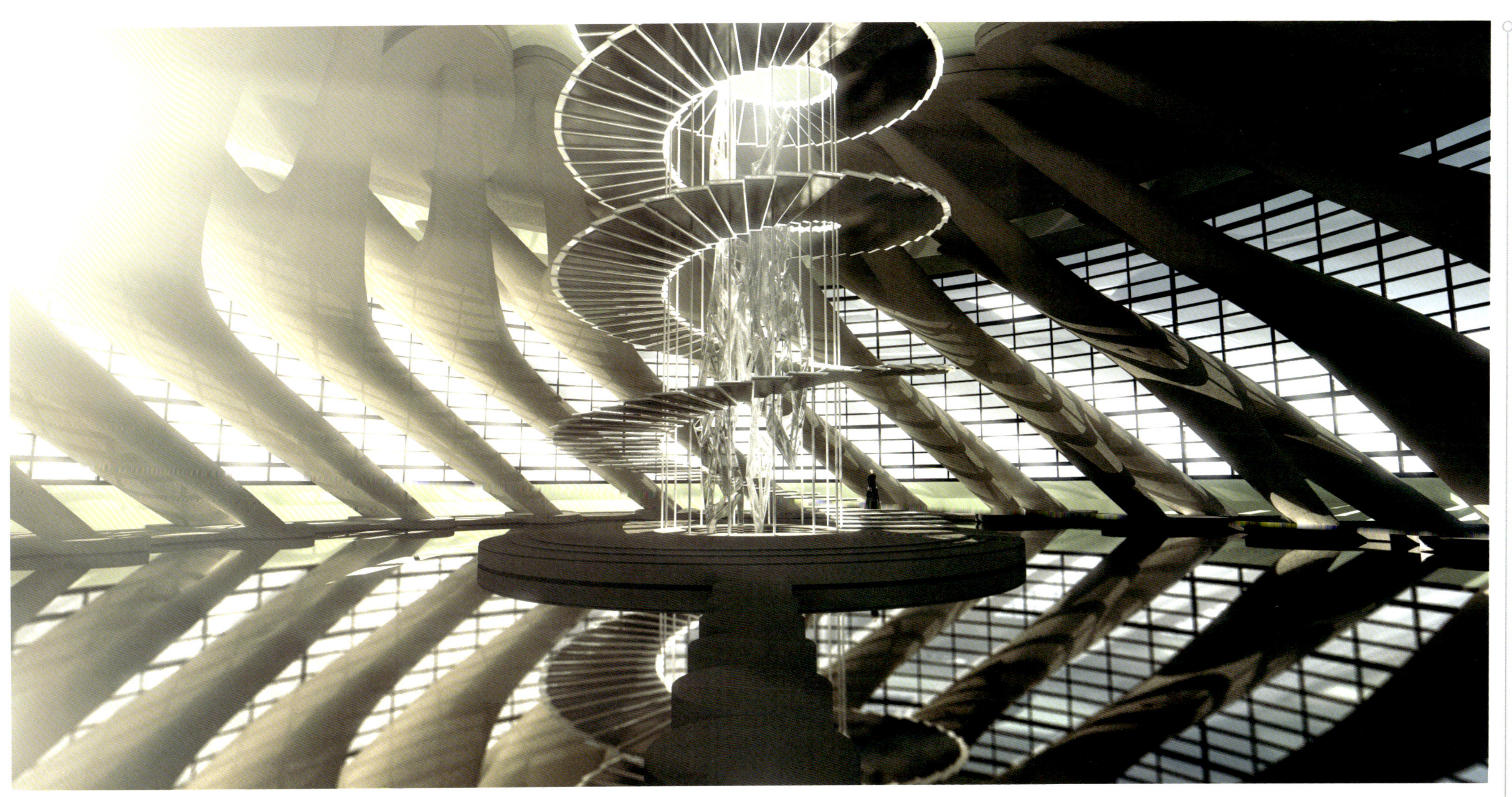

WALK TO VENTRICALLI

3000 x 1500 pixels

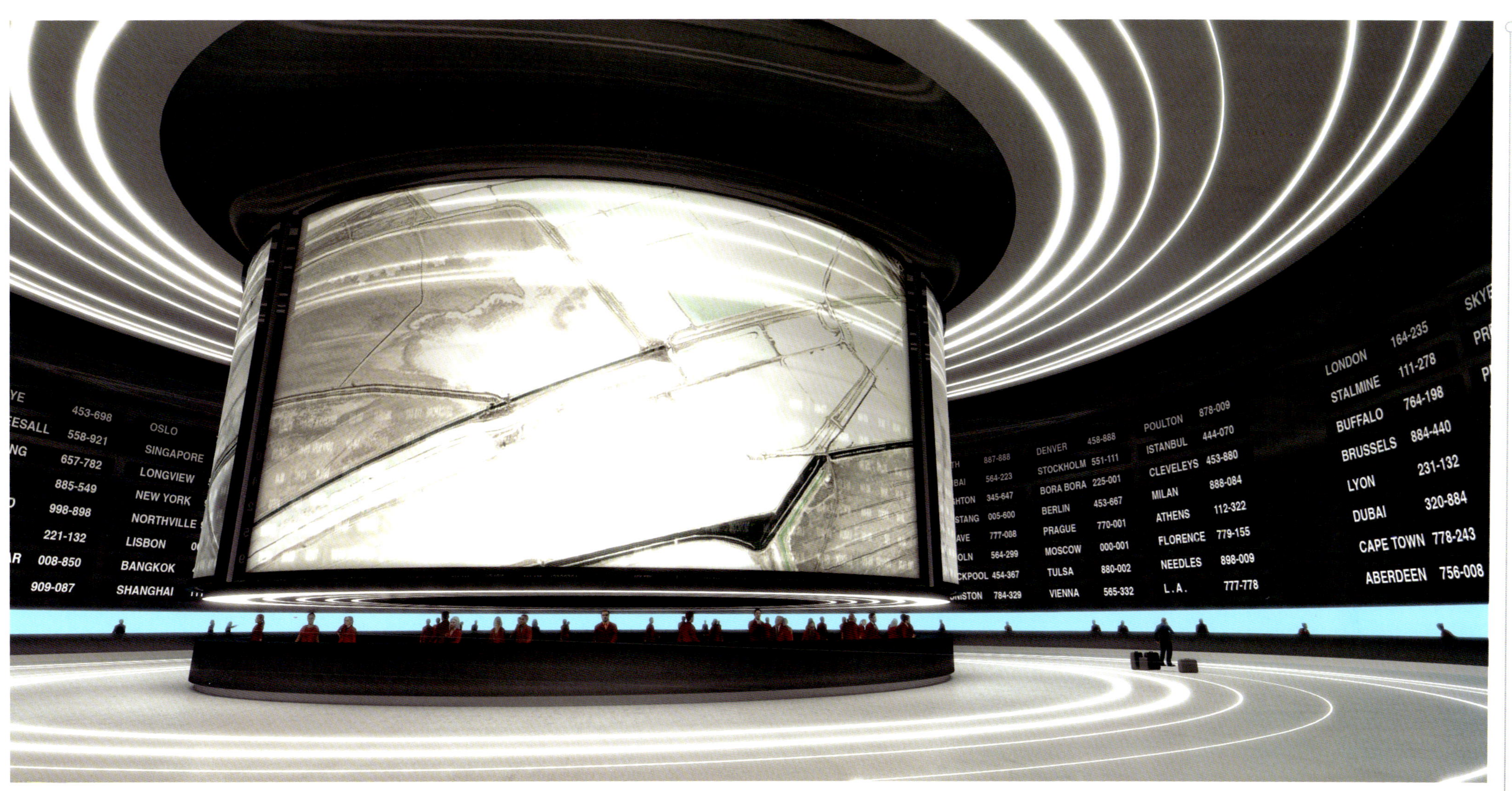

TOPOGRAPHICAL CENTER
3000 x 1500 pixels

73

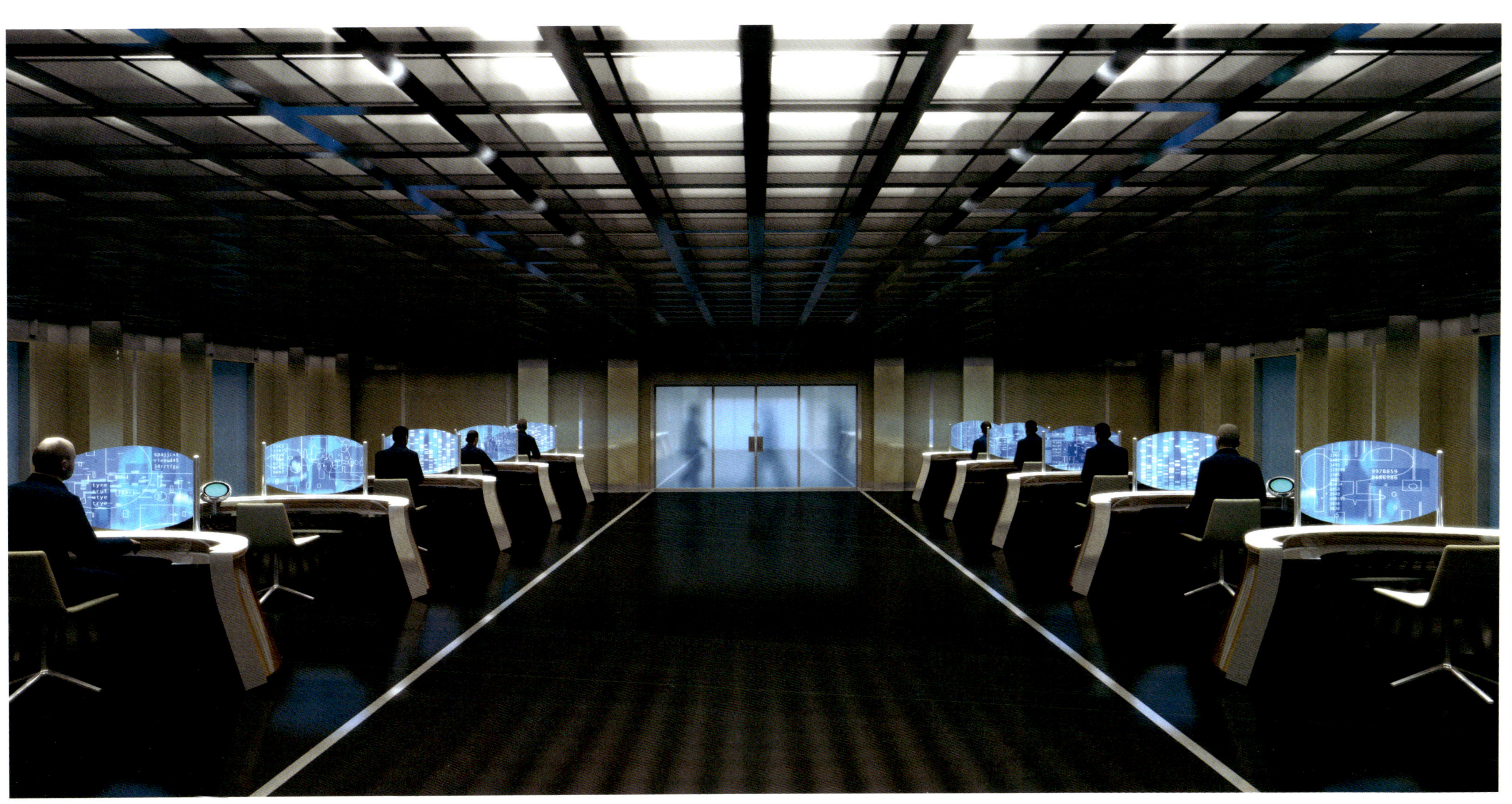

VESTRAL + 1

3000 x 1500 pixels

74

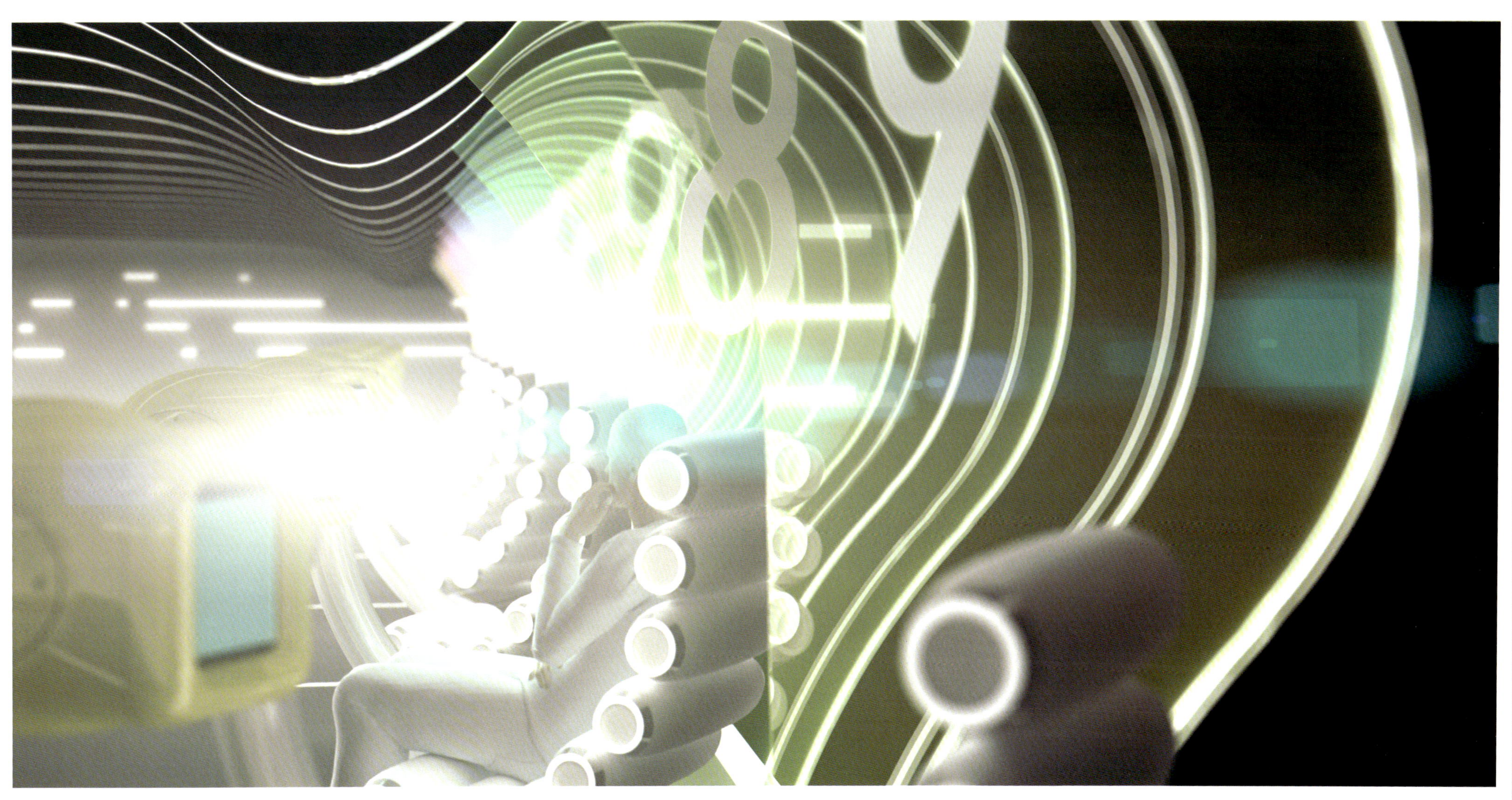

2502 x 1250 pixels

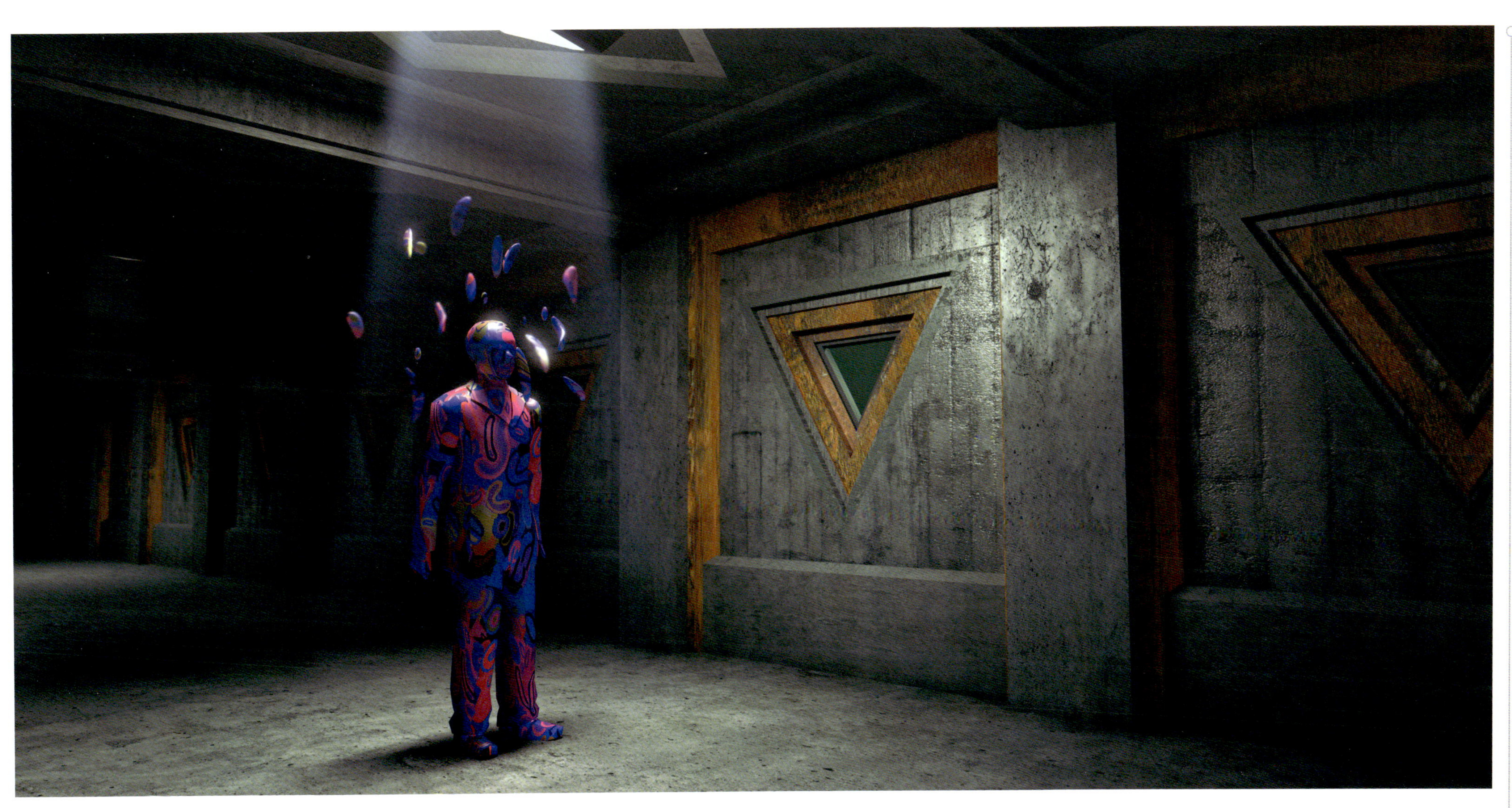

TRANSCENDENTAL
4000 x 2000 pixels

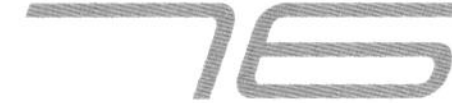

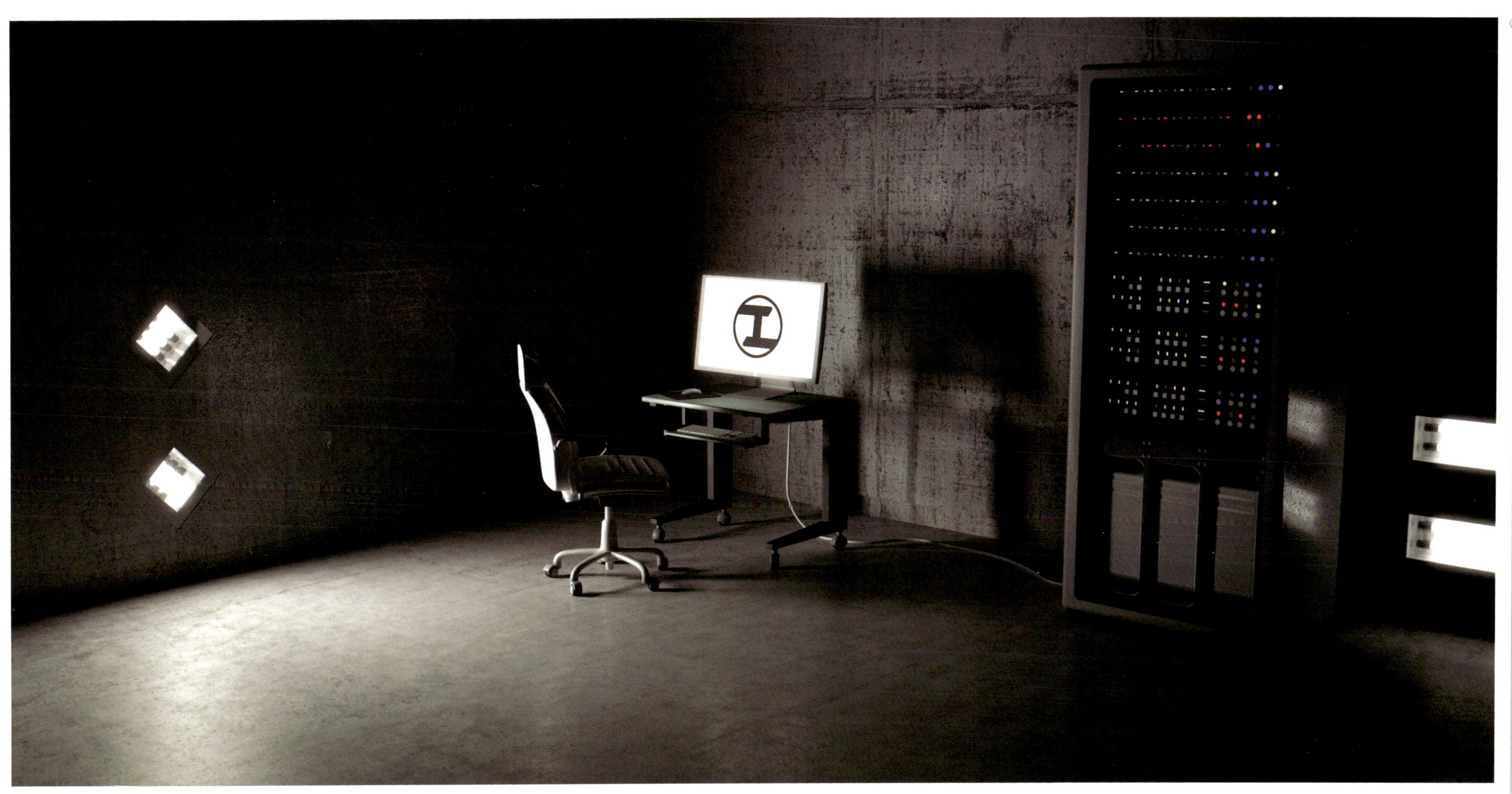

STUDIO

Seán Hargreaves was born in Blackpool, Lancashire, north England, to an engineer father and artistic mother. He lived in the green countryside of northern England until his mid-teens and then moved to the United States with his family. After studying art at the University of Houston, Hargreaves attended the prestigious Art Center College of Design in Pasadena, California, where he excelled in the field of industrial design and graduated in 1989 with a bachelor of science degree.

Hargreaves began his design career at the age of 18 in Dallas, Texas, for an engineering company that specialized in the fabrication of prototypes for Texas Instruments and others. Following his graduation at Art Center, he was hired at General Motors Advanced Concepts Center in Newbury Park, California, where he designed concept cars. It was here he learned the importance of teamwork, deadlines, and attention to detail.

After three years of designing concept cars at ACC, Hargreaves's interests turned toward the entertainment field. A close friend helped him with contacts, and before long Hargreaves was working as a storyboard artist and conceptual illustrator on commercials and film.

In the early nineties, Hargreaves's life was changed when he was hired as a concept artist on the Luc Besson–directed feature film *The Fifth Element*, working alongside famed fantasy artist Jean "Moebius" Giraud. It was in Paris that his appreciation and understanding of architecture skyrocketed and has influenced his work ever since. During his time there, Hargreaves developed an almost photorealistic style of illustration. His technique of using pen and ink, markers, and paint was relatively quick, and worked perfectly in the fast pace of the entertainment industry during a time when markers were mainly used for very fast sketches. His illustrative style of high detail, design, and lighting effectively showed directors, producers, and production designers exactly what the sets would look like. Hargreaves's style became well known and subsequently he was in high demand, sometimes working on several projects at a time.

After returning from Paris, Hargreaves worked on a number of large films with famous directors, such as *Seven* with David Fincher, *G.I. Jane* with Ridley Scott, *Heat* with Michael Mann, and *The Lost World: Jurassic Park* with Steven Spielberg. At the same time,

Hargreaves also art directed a series of music videos and commercials with production designer Tom Foden, working with prominent directors Mark Romanek and Jake Scott.

In the late nineties, Hargreaves went to work at George Lucas's Industrial Light & Magic (ILM) to design a series of high-concept commercials for a multimillion-dollar ad campaign for First Union Bank directed by Steve Beck. Hargreaves utilized all ILM had to offer in terms of visual effects. He worked for ILM for close to three years, and he has used the visual effects knowledge he gained there on many subsequent projects.

After the ad campaign, Hargreaves teamed up with director Steve Beck again to production design the feature film *Thirteen Ghosts*. The film, about a wealthy collector played by F. Murray Abraham, features the Hargreaves-designed three-level glass house, which contains the character's elaborate collection of antiques and collectables as well as ghosts. Hargreaves also production designed the film *Neverwas* for director Joshua Stern, starring Ian McKellen, Aaron Eckhart, William Hurt, and Jessica Lange.

Hargreaves has twice won the AICP Award for Production Design in commercials, and he has been nominated three times for the Art Directors Guild Award for Excellence in Production Design. His work is included in the permanent collection of the Museum of Modern Art in New York, was featured in the MoMA exhibition "Pixar: 20 Years of Animation," and appears in the books *Concept Design 2*, *The Making of Jurassic Park: The Lost World*, *Cinefex*, and others.

Hargreaves currently lives in Los Angeles, California, and works as a production designer in the entertainment industry and as a freelance design consultant.

ACKNOWLEDGMENTS:

Scott Robertson, Tinti Dey, Chris Ayers, Sandy Skora, Mike and Frances Hargreaves, Design Studio Press, Doug Trumbull, Eric Saarinen, Karim Rashid, Steve Beck, Industrial Light and Magic, Newtek.

INSPIRATION:

Matthew Barney, Santiago Calatrava, Caravaggio, Tom Foden, Jean 'Moebius' Giraud, Andreas Gursky, Mike Hargreaves, Robert Irwin, Stanley Kubrick, George Lucas, Strother McMinn, Ralph McQuarrie, Syd Mead, Oscar Neimeyer, Mark Newson, Karim Rashid, Jacques Rey, Eero Saarinen, Eric Saarinen, Ridley Scott, Doug Trumbull, James Turrell, Frank Lloyd Wright, Ted Youngkin, to name a few.

CONTACT INFO:

Seán Hargreaves can be reached by e-mail at: **seanhargreaves1@me.com**
To see more of Seán's work visit: **www.seanhargreavesdesign.com**
He can also be found on Facebook (Seán Hargreaves or Seán Hargreaves Design)

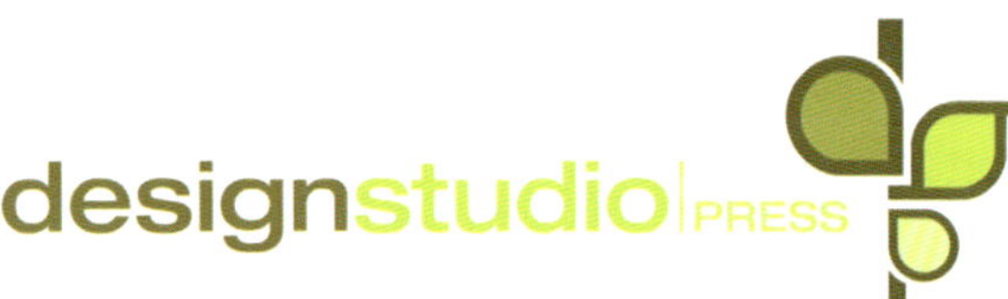

books :: limited editions :: dvds :: sales :: mailing list :: company bio :: contact :: faq :: links :: press :: cart

artist series
BATTLE MiLK 2
Counterweight
The Daily Zoo: Volume One
The Daily Zoo: Year 2
Doodles
LA ⇔ SF
Moonshine
Structura
Syd Mead's Sentury II

creatures & characters
Animals Real and Imagined
Daphne 01
Mas Creaturas
Monstruo

educational
Framed Ink
In the Future...
Luminair
The Skillful Huntsman

transportation design
Cosmic Motors
DRIVE
H-Point
Lift Off
Start Your Engines

science fiction/fantasy
Alien Race
The Colony
Concept Design 1
Concept Design 2
Entropia
Exodyssey
Quantum Dreams
Quantumscapes
Worlds

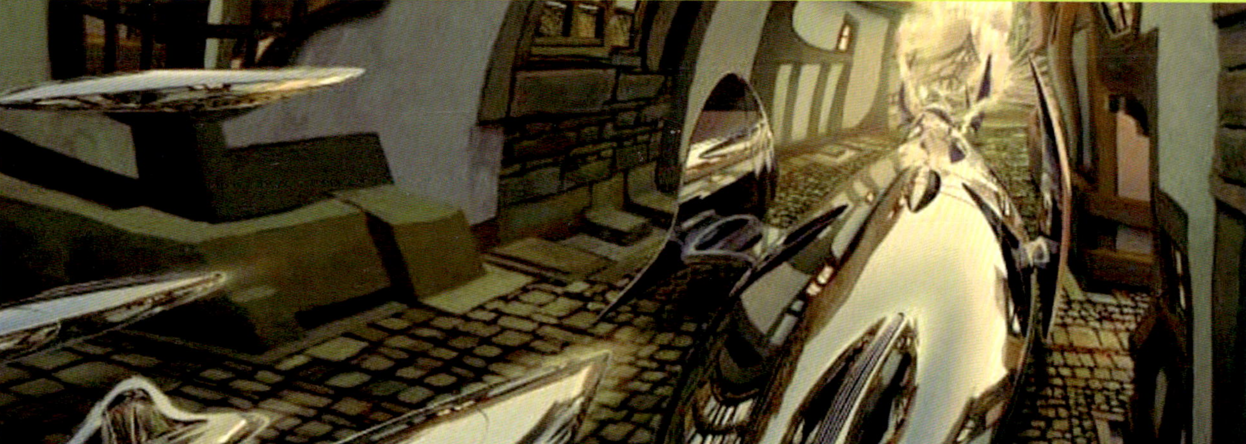

Welcome »

Design Studio Press is a specialty publisher that focuses primarily on original artistic works and educational books. We hope you enjoy the unique books we are bringing you, and this inspires you to create original images of your own. Special thanks go out to all of you who have given your kind words of encouragement to our contributing designers. The more we motivate each other to take part in the creative process the better. We hope you will support our small company so we may continue to bring original works to you far into the future.

Other DSP titles you will enjoy »

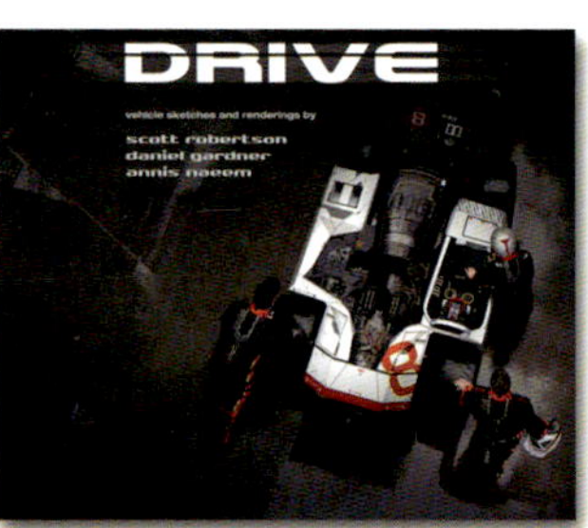

DRIVE
ISBN: 978-193349287-2

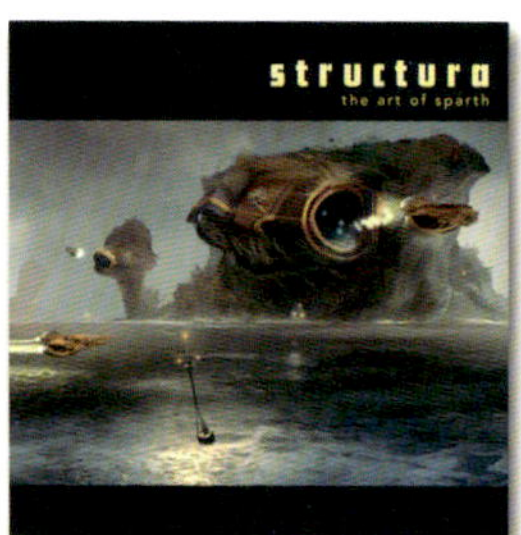

STRUCTURA
ISBN: 978-193349225-4

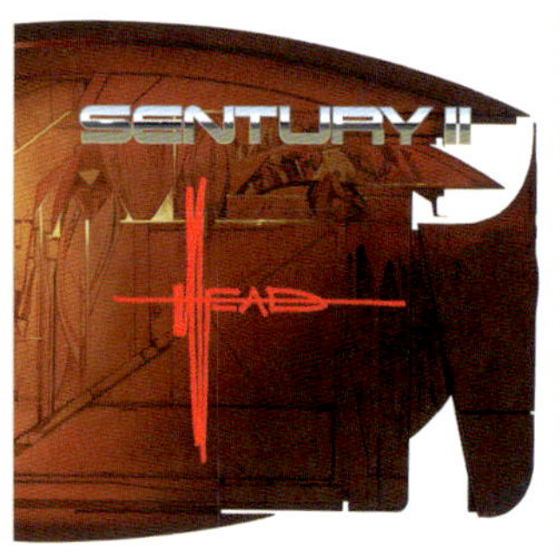

SENTURY II
ISBN: 978-193349248-3

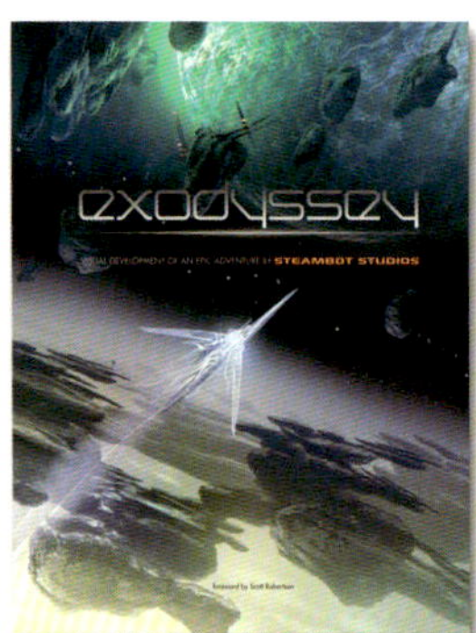

EXODYSSEY
ISBN: 978-193349239-1

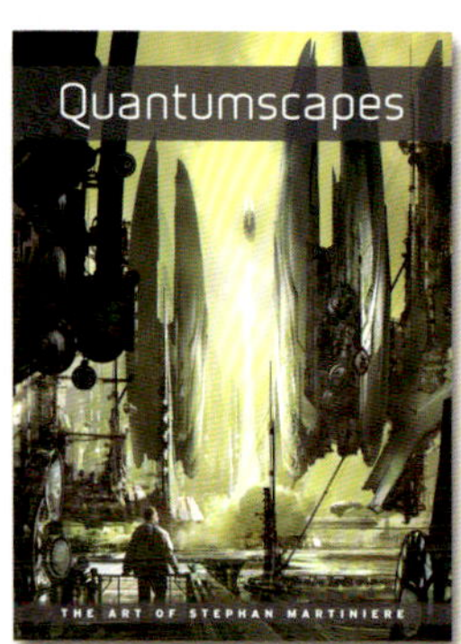

QUANTUMSCAPES
ISBN: 978-193349251-3

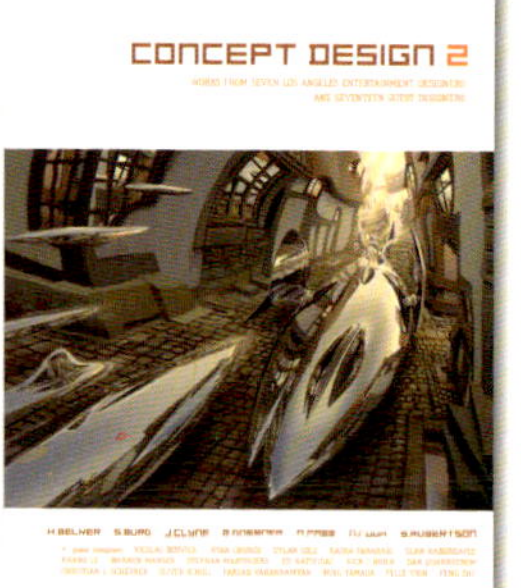

CONCEPT DESIGN 2
ISBN: 978-193349202-5

To order additional copies of this book and to view other books we offer, please visit:
www.designstudiopress.com

For volume purchases and resale inquiries, please e-mail:
info@designstudiopress.com

To be notified of special sales discounts throughout the year, please sign up to our mailing list at:
www.designstudiopress.com

Or you can write to:

Design Studio Press
8577 Higuera Street
Culver City, CA 90232

tel 310.836.3116
fax 310.836.1136